INTO THE LIGHT

A BIBLICAL APPROACH TO **HEALING FROM THE PAST**

MARY DEMUTH

LifeWay Press®
Nashville, Tennessee

Published by LifeWay Press® • © 2020 Mary DeMuth

ISBN: 978-1-0877-0594-1
Item: 005824845
Dewey decimal classification: 158
Subject heading: HEALING / HELPING BEHAVIOR / PEER
                 COUNSELING / WOMEN IN THE BIBLE

To order additional copies of this resource, write LifeWay
Church Resources Customer Service; One LifeWay Plaza;
Nashville, TN 37234; Fax order to 615.251.5933; call toll-
free 800.458.2772; email orderentry@lifeway.com; or order
online at www.lifeway.com.

Printed in the United States of America

Adult Ministry Publishing,
LifeWay Church Resources,
One LifeWay Plaza,
Nashville, TN 37234

EDITORIAL TEAM,
ADULT MINISTRY
PUBLISHING

Becky Loyd
Director, Adult Ministry

Michelle Hicks
Manager, Adult Ministry
Short Term Bible Studies

Elizabeth Hyndman
Content Editor

Erin Franklin
Production Editor

Lauren Ervin
Graphic Designer

Micah Kandros
Cover Design

CONTENTS

ABOUT THE AUTHOR

MARY DEMUTH

If you met Mary DeMuth today, her joy might confuse you. Whom she has become in light of tragedy is a testimony of Jesus' ability to transform a broken life. Mary was a child of three divorces, a victim of repeated sexual assault at five years old, and a daughter of a father who died when she was ten. Mary wanted to end her life in her teens. In the tenth grade, she heard about Jesus, and she knew she wanted to chase after Him for the rest of her life. Thankfully, He chased her.

Mary is the author of forty books, including the book this study is based on: *We Too: How the Church Can Respond Redemptively to the Sexual Abuse Crisis*. She has spoken around the world about God's ability to transform a life, bringing needed freedom to her audiences. She's the host of the popular daily podcast *Pray Every Day*, and she's been on *CNN* and featured in *The Washington Post, Christianity Today,* and *The New York Times*. She's spoken around the world in places like Munich, Johannesburg, Port-au-Prince, Geneva, and Monte Carlo, and she's planted a church with her family in southern France.

Her best work? Being a mom to three amazing young adults and the wife of twenty-nine years to Patrick. She makes her home in Dallas alongside her husband, an energetic chocolate lab, and a fuzzy black cat. Find out more at MaryDeMuth.com or WeToo.org.

INTRODUCTION

Welcome! I am proud of you. I applaud your bravery and compassion as you pick up this study. You are someone who deeply cares about the people in your life, and you understand that the God of compassion has empowered you to be empathetic toward those who are broken and walking wounded. You intrinsically understand that you, along with your brothers and sisters around the world, are the hands and feet of Jesus to those who are scattered without shepherds, who feel lost and utterly alone.

Perhaps you have felt that way too.

The overarching goal of this study, based on my book, *We Too: How the Church Can Respond Redemptively to the Sexual Abuse Crisis,* is for us to learn how to become both a good shepherd and a good Samaritan. Our time together will not specifically deal with that type of traumatic situation; instead, this study is broadened to anyone who has suffered. My prayer is we can learn how to help all the people in our lives, particularly those who are walking through struggle or trauma.

The prophet Ezekiel detailed the chastisement God had for the nation of Israel, who failed to not only proclaim God as good and in want of a relationship with the whole wide world, but also failed by treating others with unkind harshness. Consider these cautionary words in Ezekiel 34:4-6:

> You have not taken care of the weak. You have not tended the sick or bound up the injured. You have not gone looking for those who have wandered away and are lost. Instead, you have ruled them with harshness and cruelty. So my sheep have been scattered without a shepherd, and they are easy prey for any wild animal. They have wandered through all the mountains and all the hills, across the face of the earth, yet no one has gone to search for them.

What a picture of the broken today. We are a world of wanderers, untethered. Technology has simultaneously "connected" us to people all over the world while reminding us of the difficult truth: We are lonely and often alone. In isolation, predatory people prey. And in the aftermath of that preying, refugees of sadness are in desperate need of our prayers.

People need to be searched for. They bear the image of their Creator. Because of this, they are worthy of pursuit. And yet so many have struggled. They have battled family structures that neglected or perpetrated against them. They have experienced betrayal, abandonment, and contempt. And some of those injuries occurred within the four walls of the church. They long for genuine community, but their hearts are fearful. Their trust muscle has atrophied.

We can be the answer to their prayers.

Not by our strength. Not by our wits. Not by our cleverness. But by His beautiful, wooing Spirit.

This study is for them, but it is so much for you too. In order to pursue and refresh others, you must first put yourself under the spigot of God's grace. You must sit, as Mary of Bethany did, in the position of the Rabbi's disciple—at the feet of Jesus (Luke 10:39). In this place of discipleship and encouragement, you will be poured into. And from that well of overabundance, you will be able to help those who hurt.

Proverbs 11:25 reminds us, "The generous will prosper; those who refresh others will themselves be refreshed."

That is my prayer for you as you work through the next seven sessions.

Please note this study is not intended to be legal counsel or to provide holistic counseling or pastoral care on the issue of abuse. The study gives a theological foundation for healing, brings understanding on the issues connected to abuse, and gives practical wisdom by which women can navigate complex situations.

BIBLICAL FOUNDATIONS OF LOVING THE BROKEN

You don't have to venture far from your phone or the screens in your life to find pain. It's everywhere. Trauma has permeated our feeds on a micro and macro scale. Everywhere, people are suffering. It's overwhelming, and it's pervasive. And because of the fall of humankind, it's (sadly) to be expected.

When I turn through the pages of the Bible, I see a similar chaos. Violence, predation, annihilation of people groups, crucifixion, betrayal, strife within families, double crossing, war, famine, poverty, prejudice, wrath—all this within the pages of the sacred text.

These are not the passages we post on Instagram, but they are instructive. The Lord meant for the story of Job to be in the Bible, after all. Why? Because in this world we will suffer.

The entire narrative of the Bible is the story of a God who relentlessly pursues His people, despite their infidelity, waywardness, and penchant for worshipping idols and themselves. It is a divine rescue mission, inaugurated in God's mind, where He would dare leave the beauty of heaven to pitch a tent with humanity. And as He did, Jesus taught us how to love each other. He showed us what sacrifice looked like. He sought out the least, the last, and the lost because it flowed from His nature.

The life, death, and resurrection of Jesus are our coursework. How He encountered everyday people like you and me is wholly and beautifully instructive. Not only that, but the gospel is clear: Jesus not only loved us, but He fully carried out the rescue mission of the Father. He bore the weight of every one of our sins on the cross, an innocent One dying for the guilty, His blood pouring from a crowned brow of thorns. He did this for me. He did this for you. Because of love and justice.

The resurrection proved His promises, divine nature, and rescue mission. God met humanity, conquered death, and ushered in a brand-new kingdom, this age of grace we live in today.

This is the place we find ourselves, balancing like a teeter-totter between the now and the not yet. Now, we are kingdom workers seeking to love God and serve others as we bumble through life. Now, we long to see people experience the very real redemption of Jesus. Now, we are still encumbered by sin, and we have to grapple with the sad reality that people can act inhumanely toward others— yes, even in the church, yes, even when the person is a leader in the church. Now, we encounter seemingly senseless suffering as a result of our world's brokenness.

This should not be, but it is our reality. All this confusion, cover up, and pain will be vanquished gloriously on the other side, but now? We must learn what it means to live in this current world.

Jesus put it simply: "The most important commandment is this: 'Listen, O Israel! The LORD our God is the one and only LORD. And you must love the LORD your God with all your heart, all your soul, all your mind, and all your strength.' The second is equally important: 'Love your neighbor as yourself.' No other commandment is greater than these" (Mark 12:29-31).

Love God. Love others.

My hope for this week's study is that you will have a firm foundation as well as a theological construct from which to build a life that passionately loves Jesus and wisely loves those Jesus has brought into your life.

Mind if I pray for you?

Lord Jesus, would You open our eyes to Your hope for us? We need You as we look at those who are hurting. We need to understand You in the midst of the pain narrative. Help us to uncover Your empathy and make it our own, as we love those You have placed in our pathway. Reveal truth. Speak life. Renew our hearts like the dawn. Amen.

Introduce yourself to the people in your group. What drew you to this study?

How did Mary's story encourage you? How did it help you see your own pain or someone else's pain in a different light?

Describe a time when you needed the empathy of another.

What do you think it means that "an untold story never heals"? How have you seen healing in your own life or in the life of others when their stories come into the light?

What do you hope to gain from this study?

Teaching sessions available for purchase or rent at LifeWay.com/IntoTheLight

DAY ONE
THE ONE WHO NAMES GOD

When others are hurt, we naturally want to respond well. But often we don't know what to do or how to love them through their ordeals. During this first week of study, I want us to look at several passages of Scripture to demonstrate how the Bible provides a foundation as we learn to heal and help others heal from trauma.

Throughout the Bible, we see people grappling with suffering, whether physical, mental, emotional, or even social. The Bible is full of narratives, but just because a story exists within its pages does not mean the Bible promotes the behavior in the story. In other words, when we see a narrative of rape, the Bible's description of what happened is not a prescription of its permissibility, but simply a description of how a fallen people deal with trauma.

The Bible is not simply a manual of rules—to reduce it to that negates its majesty. The Word of God provides us with an abundance of stories that teach us how to navigate our world. In short, we are wired for stories. As we search the Scriptures, one of the most stunning revelations we experience is uncovering the great Story: When sin entered the world, God already had a proactive plan, one of redemption for all of us.

To be redeemed is to be bought back. Held hostage by sin, humankind cannot secure redemption, but God can and did through the life, death, and resurrection of Jesus Christ. This story informs our stories, even the ones that involve suffering. The beauty of the gospel is that it represents God's deep compassion for us all.

We see hints of the grand narrative of redemption throughout the Bible. Today, I want us to look at an unlikely heroine, Hagar.

Hagar represents so many who have been hurt by circumstances, God's people, and life. She was Sarai's maidservant, a pawn in Sarai's ploy to produce the promised offspring through conniving means. However, the moment Hagar became pregnant, Sarai despised her ability to conceive and began to mistreat her. After that, Hagar had two encounters with God that indelibly marked her. How God tenderly protected this maligned outcast is helpful to us as we seek to understand the heart and mind of a hurting person, as well as the compassionate *hesed* (loyal, covenantal love) of God toward His people.[1]

Read Genesis 15:1-6.

What did God promise to Abram? How did Abram respond?

Read Genesis 16:1-3.

What do we learn in these verses about Hagar? What plan did Sarai come up with as a solution? Why do you think she came up with that plan?

Did Hagar have a choice in the matter, from what we can tell from Scripture?

Read Genesis 16:4-6.

In your own words, what happened next in Hagar's story?

Hagar then fled to the wilderness. The New Living Translation says, "The angel of the LORD found Hagar …" (v. 7a). The angel asked her where she came from and where she was going. Hagar confessed she ran away. The angel told her to return to her mistress, and he made her a promise.

What did the angel promise in verse 10?

The angel told her to name her son Ishmael. What does his name mean?

Finish reading Genesis 16. What name did Hagar call the LORD?

What struck you as you read this biography of Hagar?

Hagar's name means "fleeing" or "flight" or "to flee."[2] We see Hagar live up to her name in two biblical accounts.

Why do you think Hagar began to treat Sarai with contempt?

Sarai blamed Abram for her problems. What does this teach us about their relationship? About Sarai's relationship with God?

We have heard the phrase, "Hurt people hurt people," and in this case, it appears to ring true. Sarai most likely carried the grief of barrenness a long time. For decades, she lived with the scorn of not being able to conceive. Being unable to conceive was considered blight from the Almighty, a judgment against someone. Without an heir, Sarai felt worthless. All that pain bottled up for so long could not help but seep out of her.

When has your grief seeped out onto another person?

Have you encountered someone who exemplified the phrase, "Hurt people hurt people"? What stuck with you from that encounter?

In this passage, Hagar ran into the angel of the LORD, who asked, "Hagar, Sarai's servant, where have you come from, and where are you going?" (v. 8a). The question revealed God's compassion and empathy toward someone who was exploited. God wanted to know her story, and He was concerned for her future.

If we would simply ask others those two questions, we'd see a revival of healing in our midst. To listen and dignify a story is freeing, and to dream about the future alongside someone who has suffered trauma is redemptive.

The angel told Hagar the name of her upcoming child: Ishmael—it means "God hears."[3] Then she became the first person in Scripture to give God a name. "Thereafter, Hagar used another name to refer to the LORD, who had spoken to her. She said, 'You are the God who sees me.' She also said, 'Have I truly seen the One who sees me?'" (v. 13).

God hears.

God sees.

When no one else does, God intervenes.[4]

Recount a time when God intervened in your life. What happened?

Throughout this study, I'll ask you to fill in charts after reading a segment of Scripture. The reason we do this is that the bulk of studying the Word of God involves seeing what is written, observing, and asking questions. This is the essence of learning biblical theology. While you read a story or passage, answering these fundamental questions will empower you for future Bible study.

Read Genesis 21:1-21.

Make six observations about the text, answering who, what, when, where, why, and how.

WHO	
WHAT	
WHEN	
WHERE	
WHY	
HOW	

When Hagar fled this second time, she and her son were starving—utterly alone, battling quiet desperation. The one who named God fell into despair. She walked away from her son who was dying of malnutrition because she couldn't bring herself to watch him die.

In that moment, God heard and saw, asked a question, and then gave a command with a promise attached. "But God heard the boy crying, and the angel of God called to Hagar from heaven, 'Hagar, what's wrong? Do not be afraid! God has heard the boy crying as he lies there. Go to him and comfort him, for I will make a great nation from his descendants'" (21:17-18).

What if we responded to broken people in a like manner? What if we dared to ask the question, "What's wrong?" while truly being interested in the person's response? What if we empathetically came alongside and gently encouraged someone away from fear and toward faith by believing them, helping them get safe, and pursuing appropriate justice for them? What if we, like the angel of the LORD to Hagar, proclaimed, prophetically, a belief in the beauty of future possibilities?

When has someone helped you move from current despair toward hope for the future?

The heart of God leans toward those who have been hurt. Consider the myriad passages about the quartet of the vulnerable (widows, orphans, foreigners, and the poor) throughout the biblical narrative. God is concerned for the downtrodden, and He punishes those who oppress the least of these.

Sadly, we think of Hagar as a blip on the Pentateuchal radar—an interesting aside. But consider this: How would we know she had radical encounters with God unless she said something to those in power? How did Moses, the writer of Genesis, know Hagar's story? We know the Word of God is inspired by God, but I also have to wonder if Hagar told others her story. She must have spoken about what she suffered and encountered.

That's the power of story.

> When have you listened to someone's story? How did it bring dignity and freedom to his or her life?

> How did listening to someone's story encourage or challenge you when facing your own suffering?

Hagar's testimony serves as an encouragement to all survivors of betrayal, exploitation, and marginalization.

God heard her. (He hears you.) God saw her. (He sees you.) God hears those who mourn. God sees those who suffer under the weight of other people's exploitation.[5]

DAY TWO
THE BLEEDING ONE

Jumping forward in the biblical narrative to the New Testament, we see another desperate person longing for change and healing. She is unnamed, but she is forever known as the woman who could not stop bleeding, the one who made her way to the Messiah and touched the fringe of His garment. What bravery she had! What moxie!

Read Luke 8:40-48.

Make six observations about the text, answering who, what, when, where, why, and how.

WHO	
WHAT	
WHEN	
WHERE	
WHY	
HOW	

I find it fascinating that the girl who would eventually be healed (Jairus's daughter) was twelve years old. The bleeding woman suffered from her condition the exact duration (twelve years) the girl had been alive.

When this woman entered the picture, she had an incurable condition. Her only hope was Jesus, so she took a huge risk by approaching Him. She was ceremonially unclean, touching the only human being on earth who was constantly, perfectly clean. And instead of defiling Him in her state, He flipped the script and cleansed her, making her whole.

When has someone flipped the script on your hurt or brokenness by engaging with you? What happened? How did his or her kindness make you feel?

Read Leviticus 15:25-27.

What does the text say about this woman's condition in relation to the purity laws?

Consider the imbalance of status in this encounter. Jesus treated both a synagogue official and an unclean woman with kindness and respect. He did not prefer one to the other; in fact, He interrupted His healing journey to pay close attention to this desperate woman. The Gospel of Mark's account uses the phrase *ousa en rhusei haimatos*, meaning "in a state of blood flow."[6] This was not a trickle, but a constant, debilitating bleed—the worst kind of heavy period that never ended.

From what we read in Scripture, how would the woman's condition have affected her everyday life?

What sort of emotions might she have experienced for twelve years?

In spite of all this, she pursued Jesus at great personal cost, but she did not approach Him from the front. The woman came up behind Jesus and gave a light touch of a tassel, a hope that healing power would bleed from Him.

According to Frank Viola, "The word for 'hem' or 'edge' in Luke is *kraspedon*,[7] and it refers to the ritual tassels commanded by Numbers 15:38-39 and Deuteronomy 22:12. She touched the tassel on the end of the square garment thrown over Jesus' left shoulder that hung down the back. (The tassels were reminders to observant Jews of God's commandments.)"[8]

Now read Mark 5:21-34.

How does the story differ from Luke's account?

According to verse 30, how was the woman healed?

According to verse 34, what is the other factor that contributed to her healing?

When we suffer, it's important to remember to have faith in God's ability to heal, trusting in His power and strength. God is capable of such a magnificent feat, but the difficulty for us all is when He chooses not to heal, not to miraculously intervene. What do we do then? And how do we help those who share that story?

We must possess comfort as Christ followers. It is the bridge between people's pain and their healing.

Read 2 Corinthians 1:3-7.

Who comforts us in our pain and worry? Why do you think so?

According to verse 5, what happens when we suffer more?

What is the point of suffering, as Paul described it in verse 6?

It's amazing our God is utterly personal, and He wants to bring us comfort. It's surprising that as our pain multiplies, God empowers us to not only endure our current trial, but He fits us with empathy so that when others suffer, we can walk alongside them.

If you have had the opportunity to help someone through pain, then describe how it felt to do so.

Why do you think God brings deep joy when you suffer alongside someone else?

Did you know that this encounter with Jesus and the woman with the issue of blood was unique? This was the only time in Scripture He called a woman His daughter. While Jairus's daughter's plight played around the corners of this story, she had a father who loved her well. But this woman appeared to have no one. Jesus, in His outrageous generosity, welcomed her as Daughter. Not a daughter, but simply Daughter. This exemplified a welcoming back into a community that had left her destitute and family-less. What a powerful example of grace Jesus gave her.

This woman personified people who suffer through no fault of their own. She did not choose her condition. She sought to be set free from it. But nonetheless, she had to endure the consequences outside of her control. Jesus gave us a beautiful pattern for how to love people in their suffering.

We turn.

We acknowledge.

We listen.

We speak healing words.

We welcome each person back to the family of God.

Pray this week the Lord will show you people to love in this way—to turn toward in their suffering, acknowledge their pain, listen to their heart, offer words of healing, and embrace them as a welcomed family member. Be alert to the possibly surprising way God will answer your prayer.

DAY THREE
IMAGO DEI

As we consider our own stories and the stories of those we love, it's important we understand theology. Theology is simply "the study of God."[9] How we think about Him, His created world and our place in it informs everything about our daily lives.

Today, we're going to look at the term *imago dei*, which is Latin for "the image of God."[10] The Hebrew term, transliterated *tzelem*, is a theological concept, which means the way God infuses dignity and special honor to those who bear His image.[11]

Genesis 1:27 reminds us of this central truth: "So God created human beings in his own image. In the image of God he created them; male and female he created them." Both men and women are image bearers, and we carry the weight of God around in our mortal bodies, the immortal shining through human skin. Because of that, we all carry weight. We matter. We are worth loving, worth being pursued, and worth being healed.

> According to Genesis 1:27, what percentage of humanity was created in God's image?

We are the result of a triune God's self-emptying love. Before our world took on soil, sky, oceans, and wildlife, our relational God existed in threefold mysterious relationship, hovering over the darkness, sufficient in Himself. He is love codified, a beautiful internal relationship that endeavored to create mankind from that harmony of fellowship. We are His children, and He is our divine parent. This thought is continued in the New Testament: "For in him we live and move and exist. As some of your own poets have said, 'We are his offspring'" (Acts 17:28).[12]

As offspring of God, every human being should be treated as the masterpiece he or she is—with dignity, protection, respect, kindness, justice, and life. Every created person is weighted with glory. No two people are alike. All have unique contributions only they can fulfill. When you encounter the death of an individual, you experience the siphoning out of one person's sweet influence. They leave a hole, and that hole can never be filled.

In light of that, how are we to live? How should we treat those who bear God's insignia?

Consider Zechariah 7:8-12:

> Then this message came to Zechariah from the LORD: "This is what the LORD of Heaven's Armies says: Judge fairly, and show mercy and kindness to one another. Do not oppress widows, orphans, foreigners, and the poor. And do not scheme against each other. Your ancestors refused to listen to this message. They stubbornly turned away and put their fingers in their ears to keep from hearing. They made their hearts as hard as stone, so they could not hear the instructions or the messages that the LORD of Heaven's Armies had sent them by his Spirit through the earlier prophets. That is why the LORD of Heaven's Armies was so angry with them."

Why do you think Zechariah referred to God as the "LORD of Heaven's Armies" (in other translations, He is the "LORD of Hosts")? How does knowing that God commands angels inform this passage?

According to this passage, what are we to do and not to do? Fill it out below.

DO	DO NOT DO

What caused the exiled nation of Israel to plug her ears to God's mandates?

Why was God furious in this passage?

Hardness of heart is a serious problem, both for the nation of Israel and for us today. With hard hearts, we desensitize to the needs of others, and we refuse to listen to the God who made them.

This is a close twin to bitterness, brought on by rebellion, yes, but also by heartache. If we have experienced heartache over and over again, and that heartache comes at the hands of those we love (or those we thought loved us), we can turn inwardly and make vows about how we will interact with the world.

Vows like:

- I will wall off my heart from everyone because no one can be trusted.
- I will limit my relationships to a small few because to risk in a new relationship is too difficult.
- I will question everyone's motives, jumping to negative intent.
- I will push God away—after all, He could have rescued me from heartache, but He did not. He is, therefore, unreliable and untrustworthy.

Have you ever made one of these vows (or a similar one)? Explain.

When we consider the powerful nature of *imago dei*, we have to understand that it extends to all—including ourselves. If it is true we are made in God's image (and that is the truth), then we, too, are worthy of respect and dignity. We, too, are loved by our Creator.

When we find ourselves in a difficult place of brokenness, we can cry out to God to heal us of that pain. Doing so gives a gift to those we love. Some may think it's selfish to take care of our hearts, but the Scripture reminds us otherwise.

Read Proverbs 4:23.

What are you tasked with in relation to your heart?

Whose responsibility is it to protect your heart?

Why do you think it is important to take care of your heart?

Why does having a healed heart matter in loving others who are also made in the image of God?

Do you have a hard time understanding that you are made in God's image and are worthy of protection? Why or why not?

Scripture describes a beautiful remedy for all of us who bear God's image.

Read Ezekiel 11:19.

What did God promise to do?

Who is the fulfillment of that promise?

Let's consider the nature of a stone. I have a little bowl of heart-shaped stones on my desk, and as I pick one up, I notice several things: it is cold, hard, and it has no life. Charles Spurgeon wrote, "According to the Word of God, man's heart is by nature like a stone; but God, through his grace, removes the stony heart and gives a heart of flesh. It is this prodigy of love, this miracle of grace, which is to engage our attention to-night."[13]

A stony heart is precisely the opposite of what we were created to be. As image bearers of God, we were created for abundant life.

Read John 10:10.

What is the purpose of a thief?

Considering that Satan is the greatest thief and the hater of every image bearer, what does he gain when we have hard hearts? How is having a hard heart a sign of our personal destruction?

On the other hand, what is Jesus' purpose?

What about your life right now exemplifies abundance and satisfaction?

Charles Spurgeon continued in his sermon about hardened hearts: "A heart of stone can bear to see its fellow creatures perish and despise their destruction; but the heart of flesh is very tender over others ... A heart of flesh would give its very life-blood if it might but snatch others from going down to the pit, for its bowels yearn and its soul moves toward its fellow sinners who are on the broad road to destruction. Have you, oh, have you such a heart of flesh as this?"[14]

Spurgeon said that when our hearts are exchanged from stone to flesh, by the powerful gospel-act of Jesus, we live with an entirely new perspective about God and the image bearers He created. Our eyes will be opened to the cries of the hurting. Our hearts bend toward those who need rescue. We won't be able to help our empathy spilling out into the lives of those who ache.

To love fellow image bearers, we must first have this necessary surgery, moving from stony heart to pliable one. We must surrender our need for control (yes, even in our relationships) to Jesus, walking toward those who are in need. We must understand intrinsically that we, too, are worthy of love and protection—by God and others.

This is internal work.

To be able to bear another's burdens, we must first have experienced Jesus bearing ours. Otherwise, in our own strength, we will burn out. What burdens do you need Jesus to bear for you? What are you trying to do in your own strength?

> Write out a prayer of surrender, asking Jesus to renew your mind, change your heart, and empower you to love the hurting people in your life.

DAY FOUR
LIGHT

We live in a dark world.

Just as parents grieve when their children hurt each other, God must grieve when His children exploit one another, assault the helpless, and traffic children. Have you considered the grief of God as He looks upon this earth? How His heart must ache from our choices! We see the grief of God prior to the flood when the earth was filled with unrelenting violence (Gen. 6:6). God's heart throughout the history of the nation of Israel was to woo humanity back to Himself, a relationship that was forever altered in the garden when the first human beings chose the lure of knowing good and evil over relationship with the only One who was good (Gen. 3). Israel was to be a light shining in the darkness, a vehicle for bringing a broken humanity back to the One who created her.

Attention to the imagery of light reveals the story of God throughout the Testaments, and this frequent metaphor peppers the pages of Scripture. Prior to the creation of humanity, God said, "'Let there be light,' and there was light" (Gen. 1:3). Post flood, God inaugurated His first great commission when He called Abraham to leave his home and become a great nation (Gen. 12). Throughout the Old Testament, we see admonitions that this new nation was to protect the helpless, care for the poor, support the widow, and extend kindness to foreigners. This power differential that existed in the world was not intended for exploitation, but service. Those who found themselves in positions of power were to judge fairly, love widely, and create a just society. All this hinted at a future glory, when God Himself would send the Son to continue this practice publicly.[15]

The nation of Israel was tasked to be a light to the world. "You will do more than restore the people of Israel to me. I will make you a light to the Gentiles, and you will bring my salvation to the ends of the earth" (Isa. 49:6). You can almost taste the groaning of God in this passage, this great unveiling of the progression of His plan of salvation. "Arise, Jerusalem! Let your light shine for all to see. For the glory of the LORD rises to shine on you. Darkness as black as night covers all the nations of the earth, but the glory of the LORD rises and appears over you. All nations will come to your light; mighty kings will come to see your radiance" (Isa. 60:1-3).

This light-bearing mandate prepared Israel to meet her King, Jesus. Isaiah prophesied, "The people who walk in darkness will see a great light. For those who live in a land of deep darkness, a light will shine" (Isa. 9:2).

That light did shine in the person of Jesus Christ.

Read John 1:1-5.

In what ways do we see the Trinitarian nature of God in this passage?

Who brings the Light to this world?

What is the promise we find at the end of this passage? How does that give you hope today?

We can see the power of light in play in the story of the man born blind and his interaction with Jesus.

Read John 9.

Make six observations about the text, answering who, what, when, where, why, and how.

WHO	
WHAT	
WHEN	
WHERE	
WHY	
HOW	

This man's blindness is a helpful metaphor for those who are hurting. Why? Because he didn't cause his blindness. The disciples, seeking to understand the cause of his blindness, asked an insensitive question about why the man had the condition. Was it his fault? His parents? Jesus responded that it was neither of those scenarios.

Why did Jesus say the blind man was born blind?

Do you think this is true whenever Christians suffer? Why or why not?

We may never know the reason why we experience certain hurts and suffering. We, after all, cannot shed a light on human hearts, nor should we presume to know motives. Some of the most painful interactions trauma survivors experience is the questioning by well-meaning people. Sexual abuse survivors, in particular, have heard many insensitive words. They often hear questions and statements like:

- What were you wearing?
- Are you sure it happened?
- How did you contribute?
- Have you forgiven?
- Why did you put yourself in that situation?
- Why didn't you fight back?
- How come it took you so long to report?
- That was a long time ago. You should be over it by now.

We have to remember that when people are sinned against, the shame belongs to the one who perpetrated, but the victimized often internalize that shame. Through listening and asking kindhearted questions, we may become aware of the lies our friends now believe because of their pain. In a loving, non-judgmental manner we can help them see the truth—that in the midst of the pain, God still loves them. He still accepts them. He still pursues them.

This is the power of listening first, then asking questions. We cannot know what is in someone's heart, but we are more likely to understand if we stay quiet, listen to his or her story, and then tenderly ask questions as God leads. These are the kinds of conversations that change lives.

How does Jesus' healing of the man born blind encourage you?

Reread the end of the passage in John 9:35-41.

What was the man's response to learning the identity of Jesus (v. 38)?

What does Jesus equate blindness with in verse 41?

Before you met Jesus, how were you blind?

That's a perfect bridge to interact with Ephesians 5:6-14, which highlights darkness and sin:

> Don't be fooled by those who try to excuse these sins, for the anger of God will fall on all who disobey him. Don't participate in the things these people do. For once you were full of darkness, but now you have light from the Lord. So live as people of light! For this light within you produces only what is good and right and true. Carefully determine what pleases the Lord. Take no part in the worthless deeds of evil and darkness; instead, expose them. It is shameful even to talk about the things that ungodly people do in secret. But their evil intentions will be exposed when the light shines on them, for the light makes everything visible. This is why it is said, "Awake, O sleeper, rise up from the dead, and Christ will give you light."

As light bearers, what is our responsibility in terms of the darkness?

We are to expose darkness, becoming like "a city on a hilltop" (Matt. 5:14), shining a beacon of hope and healing into the dark of sin. This is not an easy task or one we should take lightly.

Think about a time when you exposed the darkness about something, or perhaps you were just witness to someone else exposing darkness. What happened? How did exposing the darkness change the circumstances for those involved?

Why do you think it's difficult to expose darkness? What does it cost someone to put a spotlight on evil?

How has Jesus shed light in your life? In your relationships?

We can become overwhelmed by our problems, the darkness of this world, and the plight of others. When we do, it's important to embrace eschatological living, which simply means to live in light of what will be, when the new heaven and the new earth dawn.[16]

Perfect justice does not yet exist on this earth, though we try to work toward that. Perfect love is elusive. But one day, all will be well, justice will be meted out, and our tears will be wiped away. The prophet Isaiah hinted at that day:

> No longer will you need the sun to shine by day, nor the moon to give its light by night, for the LORD your God will be your everlasting light, and your God will be your glory. Your sun will never set; your moon will not go down. For the LORD will be your everlasting light. Your days of mourning will come to an end. All your people will be righteous. They will possess their land forever, for I will plant them there with my own hands in order to bring myself glory. The smallest family will become a thousand people, and the tiniest group will become a mighty nation. At the right time, I, the LORD, will make it happen.
> ISAIAH 60:19-22

The fulfillment of that vision culminates in Revelation 21:22-25. It reads:

> I saw no temple in the city, for the Lord God Almighty and the Lamb are its temple. And the city has no need of sun or moon, for the glory of God illuminates the city, and the Lamb is its light. The nations will walk in its light, and the kings of the world will enter the city in all their glory. Its gates will never be closed at the end of day because there is no night there.

One day Jesus will be all the light we need. Darkness will be vanquished.

How does reminding yourself about the future glory help you persevere today?

Why is it important to have an eternal perspective on things?

Our lives are a pinprick in time, but eternity extends forever. With an eternal perspective, our short time on earth becomes important. How we love matters. How we deal with evil and pain matters. How we expose the darkness matters.

With a proper theology of light, we remember that the darkness ultimately will not win. Sometimes we need to remind ourselves of that beautiful truth. Sometimes we need to remind others.

Who comes to mind when you think of someone who is battling the darkness? Stop and say a prayer for that person today.

DAY FIVE
JESUS

Jesus said, "I am the light of the world. If you follow me, you won't have to walk in darkness, because you will have the light that leads to life" (John 8:12).

When we want to understand how to love the hurting in our midst, we have to look to Jesus to see how to live. He encountered many suffering people in His sojourn on earth. Even in His death, He revealed to us how to suffer well.

Jesus was both silent and loquacious when He faced torture and mocking. He stood silent in the Synoptic Gospels (Matthew, Mark, and Luke), spotlighting His connectedness to the Suffering Servant mentioned in Isaiah 53:7—"He was oppressed and treated harshly, yet he never said a word. He was led like a lamb to the slaughter. And as a sheep is silent before the shearers, he did not open his mouth." Yet in the Book of John, we see His response to the high priest: "Everyone knows what I teach. I have preached regularly in the synagogues and the Temple, where the people gather. I have not spoken in secret. Why are you asking me this question? Ask those who heard me. They know what I said" (John 18:20-21). Jesus went on to interact with Pilate as well.

Why bring up this distinction? Because some, horrifically, have used Jesus' silence in the face of suffering as a prescription for abuse survivors, telling them that it is godly to keep abuse silent. The latter interactions in John undermine this argument, and if anything, Jesus' words, "I have not spoken in secret," refute this silencing takeaway.[17]

Telling our stories to safe people is the first step toward healing. Consider how many times Jesus drew out people on the margins of life. He asked questions. He listened. He was interested. This holy curiosity informed the way He loved folks as He walked the dusty roads of Jerusalem and its surrounding communities.

When have you told a difficult story to a safe person? What happened?

When has someone entrusted a painful story to you? How did you feel as they shared?

Can you recall one of the most significant conversations you've had? What happened? What made the interaction memorable?

Read John 8:1-11, the story of the woman caught in adultery.

Make six observations about the text, answering who, what, when, where, why, and how.

WHO

WHAT

WHEN

WHERE

WHY

HOW

Read Leviticus 20:10.

According to Old Testament law, who should be punished for adultery, and how? Why is this significant to the story above?

Whenever Jesus interacted with the broken, He surprised people. The Law indicated death for this woman, but she walked away wholly alive. And in the midst of that, the surrounding people received a poignant object lesson. Jesus is both grace and truth. We see grace as she lived, and we see truth when Jesus told her to refrain from sin from that point forward.

Jesus, the only perfect One, had the right to enact justice, but He chose a different path. He cleared the way for a brand new life of grace.

He does that for all of us. His life, death, and resurrection beckon us to a new life, a gospel-centered dance, where we are now called ambassadors, helping others have a brand new life.

Will we suffer on this earth? Yes. Will we fall? Yes. Will we face discouragement? Yes. Will people betray us? Yes. But because we have the Holy Spirit within us, we have all that we need to endure with joy.

The Book of Philippians has joy at its roots. In Philippians 2:5-8 we see the paradoxical reason for Jesus' joy. It's a Greek word: **kenosis**.[18]

> "You must have the same attitude that Christ Jesus had. Though he was God, he did not think of equality with God as something to cling to. Instead, *he gave up his divine privileges*; he took the humble position of a slave and was born as a human being. When he appeared in human form, he humbled himself in obedience to God and died a criminal's death on a cross" (emphasis mine).

Though God, Jesus didn't accept the privileges that came with being God. Instead, He let go of those privileges for the sake of giving us a tangible example of love. To love another is to pour out. To love is to consider someone else more important than ourselves. To love is to lay down our lives and serve another's interests. Think about the audacity of **kenosis** for a moment. In a world where men and women claw their way to power and prominence, Jesus, who already had it, gloriously let it go.[19]

How does understanding the *kenosis* of Jesus empower you to serve someone who is struggling?

Read Luke 19:1-10 about Zacchaeus.

Who was Zacchaeus? What had he done before meeting Jesus?

Zacchaeus could be considered a predatory person before he met Jesus. He preyed upon the less fortunate to line his own pockets, causing hurt, poverty, and suffering.

Why do you think Zacchaeus wanted to see Jesus?

What does restoration look like in this passage?

Zacchaeus promised to change. How do we know he truly changed?

We don't see Zacchaeus give all his money back in this passage of Scripture. However, we know from the One who sees our hearts and knows our minds that Zacchaeus had truly changed. Repentance that is merely words is not repentance at all. Repentance has teeth. It restores. It not only admits wrong, but it seeks to right those wrongs. This is vitally important to understand for two reasons:

1. Predatory people are very good at saying Christian words but seldom back those words up with restorative action. We must become better at discerning them.

2. Those who have been harmed may feel a predatory person's words are confusing. They may need your help in unpacking their emotions and worries. So often they've been told to forgive quickly without any measurable repentance.

Repentance in word only is empty.

Repentance with right action over a period of time indicates that there is a possibility that relationship can be restored.

Recall a time when someone's words of repentance (I'm sorry) were *not* followed by restorative action. How did that make you feel? What happened in the long term?

What does the story of Zacchaeus teach you about a changed life?

In the case of Zacchaeus, there is no doubt about his repentance. In this moment, his words matched his actions, and those actions were extreme. This is why Jesus said salvation has come to his house and life. As people who want to bear the weight of another's story, we can look to this passage for hope; it is possible for people to experience life change.

Jesus, the Light of the world, was curious about others. He helped those who were hurting share their stories. He offered a grace-infused response to those who struggled. He emptied Himself of rightful fame in order to identify with us. He revealed what a life changed by the gospel looked like in His interaction with Zacchaeus. Because of this, we do not have to wander aimlessly as we strive (through the power of the Holy Spirit) to love others. We have a roadmap, and not only that, but Jesus beautifully walked that map. His tangible example of love pouring out empowers us to pour out His love on others. What a privilege!

THIS WEEK'S WE TOO MOMENT

Each week you'll see a "We Too Moment" to help you act on what you've learned throughout the week of study. These are optional, but I hope they'll bless you as you are challenged.

Read Matthew 5:3-10.

> God blesses those who are poor and realize their need for him,
> for the Kingdom of Heaven is theirs.
> God blesses those who mourn,
> for they will be comforted.
> God blesses those who are humble,
> for they will inherit the whole earth.
> God blesses those who hunger and thirst for justice,
> for they will be satisfied.
> God blesses those who are merciful,
> for they will be shown mercy.
> God blesses those whose hearts are pure,
> for they will see God.
> God blesses those who work for peace,
> for they will be called the children of God.
> God blesses those who are persecuted for doing right,
> for the Kingdom of Heaven is theirs.

God blesses you when people mock you, and persecute you, and lie about you, and say all sorts of evil things against you because you are His followers. Be happy about it! Be very glad! For a great reward awaits you in heaven. And remember, the ancient prophets were persecuted in the same way.

Now read this wearing the lens of someone in your life who is suffering.

How does seeing this passage through his or her eyes change your experience of Jesus' words?

ACTION: Choose one of these verses, or perhaps the whole passage, write it out, and send it to a struggling friend. (And yes, I mean a card, an envelope, a stamp, and the mail.)

EXAMPLE: "I was reading through the Sermon on the Mount this week, and verse 4 stood out to me: "God blesses those who mourn, for they will be comforted." It reminded me of your grief of late, and how difficult it must be for you as you mourn what was lost. This verse reminds us both that comfort will come. I pray it will arrive tangibly this week. I'm so sorry for what you've been walking through, and I wish I could take it all away from you (and I'm sure you would rather not be walking through it). May God's comfort put breath back into your lungs. Please know I am praying toward that end. I love you, [NAME]."

THE ANATOMY OF THE HEALING JOURNEY

We are all on a healing journey, whether we've suffered abuse in the past or not. This life is not easy, and it is full of disappointments, moments of glory and despair, and fighting against darkness. How do we get to a healthy place? How do we find solace? As Christ followers, we pray. We seek God through the Scriptures. But we also need each other.

The header of WeToo.org simply states, "We heal better together." We heal best in community with others, with brothers and sisters daring to carry our burdens. Hebrews 10:25, an oft-quoted verse, reminds us of the importance of being with other believers. "And let us not neglect our meeting together, as some people do, but encourage one another, especially now that the day of his return is drawing near." Community, though risky, is a genuine benefit for the struggling one.

Seldom do we heal in isolation. In my own life, when I sequester myself away from others, my soul atrophies; I believe so many lies unchecked, and my depressive thoughts border on obsessive.

I need others. I need to tell my story. I need to know I was not crazy.

My story is not an easy one, but because of the body of Christ bearing my burdens and praying me toward health, it is a good one now.

I grew up in a home I would not want to duplicate. A child of three divorces, neglect, yearlong sexual abuse at five, drug use in the home, and a parental death (my biological father), I suffered much, and I suffered alone. As an only child, I longed for a safe place. The only safety I eventually found came through friendships. This would be the foundation God would build on later to help me pursue godly relationships.

But because of the weightiness of heartache, I faced a lot of fear. Would this next person I trusted be kind to me or exploit me? Sometimes I made terrible relational decisions because my upbringing didn't prepare me to choose wisely. My fallback was to choose highly dysfunctional friends and mentors because that is precisely what felt normal to me. Only as I grew in my relationship with Christ did I begin to understand how to choose safe, kindhearted people as friends.

You may be in that place, too. You may be afraid to trust again. Your backpack of betrayal may be heavy upon your shoulders, and you fear adding another weight to carry. The paradoxical (and sometimes frustrating) truth is this: We are broken in community, but God beckons us toward health in community. What has wounded is what heals. Bad interactions may have left you reeling, but finding sweet, encouraging friendships can release you from bitterness and fear. That is why the healing journey is sheer risk.

You may be thinking that it's selfish to pursue your own healing. But it's not. To pursue your healing journey is to love the people God has placed in your life. A healed heart is powerful. You can bear more burdens if your pain burden is lightened. If you cannot heal for yourself, choose to pursue it for the sake of those you love.

Once a woman came up to me after a talk I gave. She detailed the pain she had in her relationship with her mother, who, in her seventies, finally disclosed past sexual abuse. But prior to that disclosure, their relationship was fraught with pain, particularly her mother wounding her and her family.

I asked her this simple question: "Would it have been a gift to you had your mother pursued healing earlier?"

She burst into tears. "Yes," she said. "It would have changed everything."

That's my heart for you this week. To boldly chase healing for yourself so you can be the kind of person others pursue. To be set free so you can become an emancipator of others.

Mind if I pray for you?

Jesus, we need healing. We choose to welcome it. We choose to tell our stories. We need light and life and hope. Would You provide all three in abundance? Show us the healing path before us, and help us not to shrink from it in fear. Give us faith to trust You through the process. And please teach us how to bear the burdens of those in our lives today. Amen.

The journey begins with a story.

VIEWER GUIDE
SESSION TWO

Which of the pits Mary discussed in the video is closest to the one(s) you've experienced or seen in the lives of those you love? How so?

Mary said, "You are rescued to be a rescuer." How have you seen that be true in your own life or in the lives of those who have helped rescue you?

There is a so-what and a now-what to your story. What does that mean? If you're comfortable doing so, share your so-what and now-what with the group. It's OK if you don't know it yet. Pray God will reveal it to you.

How does knowing that God jumps in the pit with you give you hope, no matter your situation?

Teaching sessions available for purchase or rent at LifeWay.com/IntoTheLight

NOTES

DAY ONE
STORIES

The Bible is a complicated yet cohesive work. Poetry, outcries, imprecatory prayers, prophecy, apocalyptic discourse, laments, and, yes—stories. So many stories. And they're not all prettified. Murder, rape, betrayal, denial, coercion, war, broken families—it's all there, stark on the page. We do the Bible a disservice by dissecting it into manageable bites, stitching happy verses on pillows while skipping over the unsavory parts.

But we need the unsavory parts.

Our stories, too, are complicated, seldom linear, often stormy. When we read about the failings of others on the pages of the Bible, we find a strange camaraderie. We are frail people, seeking an empowering God. We realize we need a Savior.

This is the beauty of the Bible—the great story arc of Scripture. All was pristine and beautiful in the garden where God planted the first man and woman. But Satan slithered into the idyllic space, tempting humankind to sin. In that dark moment of human decision, everything changed. Nakedness exposed. Death introduced. Brokenness established.

But this is not where the story ended. God, the Storyteller, already forethought a plan to redeem us all. He chose a people, the nation of Israel, to beckon humanity to Himself. The Israelites were to be a light on the hill, showing the world His beauty and character. But, as you know, they (just like we would do) bumbled their mandate. They wandered. They faltered. They shrunk back from divine callings. They weathered the cycle of the judges, demanded kings who rose and fell, and found themselves exiled from their promised land where the temple lay in ruins. As the ragtag bunch returned, they were still looking for rescue—for a king to redeem them.

When Jesus broke through the narrative of humankind, He was an unlikely hero. A carpenter's Son of dubious heritage, He started His ministry by blessing a wedding party with wine, and then called others to follow Him. He healed those with diseases, cast out demons, and taught about a new kingdom. He lived the perfect life that sin-stained humanity could not. This King died in a disgraceful manner, as a criminal upon a Roman cross.

If that's all there was to the story, you would not be reading these words today.

The resurrection was proof of Jesus' deity, His conquering of sin, and rescuing of humanity. He vanquished the curse of shame and death brought on by our ancestors. The veil in the temple, which separated humanity from God, was torn in two from top to bottom as if God Himself ripped it from heaven.

As we believe this gospel, this good news, we are ushered into an entirely new story. No longer entrenched in sin. No longer exiled from God. No longer suffering from the weight of all we have done wrong, we stand blessedly forgiven. Not only that, we are adopted into a new family. We are now children of God.

But wait! There's more. We who struggle to live a life of joy and patience now have a priceless gift. The very Spirit of God resides in us, His new temple. This is good news. We are no longer enslaved to sin but are now servants of righteousness. And as kingdom workers, we have the privilege of sharing our stories with the rest of the world, ushering in bits and pieces of His kingdom until that final day when everything will be made right.

This is the grand narrative we find ourselves in today. This is the gospel.

If someone were to ask you, "What is the gospel?," what would you say? How would you explain it?

This is the most powerful story that trumps all other stories.

We, too, have a story. We have a beginning (inciting incident), a middle full of rising action and conflict, and, eventually, we will have a climax, the denouement (resolution) happening on heaven's shores. This story matters because, as God's beloved children, we matter.

We learned last week about Hagar's interaction with El Roi, "the God who sees" (Gen. 16:13). He also sees your story. He cares about your journey.

Look at the simple diagram on the next page. This is the story arc.

On the diagram, list the following:

- Your birthday
- Any significant events of your life so far (on the rising line)
- Make today the climax (top of pyramid).
- On the right hand side, list three ways you would like to grow from this point forward.

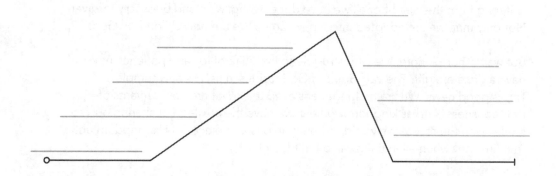

Sometimes it's difficult to recount the past. Often I have told audiences, "an untold story never heals." This may be the first time you've looked at your life in its totality on the page. But it's the first step in healing.

Some of us are really afraid for others to know what goes on in our hearts and minds. Some of us have become adept at tamping down our pain to make ourselves more palatable to the world. Some are terrified of secrets being let out, not simply because we are ashamed, but because that secret might topple our family, church, or job.

Let's look at one story of a man Jesus encountered who suffered many years without relief.

Read John 5:1-15

Make six observations about the text, answering who, what, when, where, why, and how.

WHO	
WHAT	
WHEN	
WHERE	
WHY	
HOW	

What question did Jesus ask the paralyzed man?

What was the man's response? Why couldn't he get well?

What day did this happen? Why is that significant?

Did the man truly answer Jesus' question about wanting to get well? No. He made an excuse (a good one). He couldn't make it into the water to find healing. He had limitations. But he never said, "Yes, Jesus, I want to be free of this problem. I want to get well."

Our gracious Savior didn't penalize the man for not answering the question. Instead, He offered grace in the form of surprising healing. He did this to rescue the man and display His ability to heal, as well as give glory to God. How sweet of Jesus to not make answering a question correctly be the gateway to healing.

So often we see a formulaic view of Christianity creep into our churches. We teach people a form of the prosperity gospel that goes something like, "Say this correctly-worded prayer, repent this way, do these good things, and God is obligated to answer your prayer in the manner you want Him to."

Sadly, life and the kingdom do not work out this way.

God is sovereign, which means He chooses to act according to His nature and His plan. One hundred percent of us will die, many from diseases we will no doubt pray for release from. Many of us walk through suffering to the other side; we are not often delivered immediately from difficult circumstances. The promise Jesus gives us is not "never get sick" or "no more problems."

Read John 16:33.

What does Jesus promise us?

How is that comforting today?

Jesus asks us that same question: Do you want to get well? As I mentioned earlier, part of the healing process is learning to recount our stories to safe people. Letting our stories out into the light evaporates the power that darkness and lies hold over us.

If you long to be the kind of person who can love your friends and family well, working on your own story is necessary work. You cannot ask others to go where you have not yet trekked.

Here's the pattern.

You go first so others can say, "Me too."

Tell your story. Give someone else the privilege of bearing the weight of your story. And then take up your mat and walk, praising and glorifying God.

DAY TWO
SECRETS

I remember having to keep two secrets in childhood.

Secret one. I kept the sexual assault I experienced at five years old by neighborhood teens quiet for a period of time. They told me if I told anyone, they would kill my parents. For several months, I kept that secret. It wasn't until they began telling their friends to join them that I mustered the courage to tell my babysitter what happened. She told me she would tell my mom, and I believed her.

The following day, I let out a breath. I would no longer have to be assaulted! But the boys knocked on her door again, and she forced me outside. I thought my mom knew and didn't care. This was devastating to me.

Secret two. This one is more pervasive. No one in my family threatened me, but we had this unwritten code of silence in our family system. We simply did not talk about what went on if it was negative. I was only permitted to exhibit positive emotions, and I could not complain publicly about what was happening behind closed doors.

I can recall the first time I shattered that silence. I sat in my grandparents' living room, utterly broken. I was a young teen facing my mother's third divorce on Father's Day. My biological father died when I was ten, so my third father (second stepdad) became everything to me. He and my mother sat in my grandparents' living room. Without realizing it, suddenly I was weeping. My mom chastised me for crying, then my grandmother whisked her away to the kitchen while my tears unleashed. It felt like a scene from the children's story about the emperor having no clothes—suddenly the obvious was in the open. I would lose yet another father.

My telling of the truth was disruptive. But it also set me free. Yes, my mourning was messy, but as long as I kept that secret, my heart atrophied. Speaking up in that moment was excruciating. I feared I would ruin everything. (And my instinct was correct in many ways. I certainly got in trouble for sharing). But a bit of myself was healed in the light.

A year or so later I would meet Jesus Christ. My broken heart would begin the arduous process of being put back together. And I would learn over and over again that the kind of secrets I thought I had to keep silent would break me. Only when I let them out would freedom begin.

In your family, did you have secrets or expectations about what could and could not be shared?

When was the first time you remember letting out a secret? What happened?

The opposite of harboring secrets is being set free by Jesus to tell the truth. Let's look at some Scriptures throughout the Bible that underscore this truth.

Read Psalm 15:2.

What does it mean in your daily life to speak the truth from a sincere heart?

Read Proverbs 12:17.

What does a false witness do? Why?

Read Zechariah 8:16-17.

Why is it important that a court system render truth-filled verdicts?

Read Ephesians 4:14-15,25.

Practically, what is the difference between speaking the truth in love versus speaking it with ill intention? Share an example of both situations on the next page.

1. Truth in love:

2. Truth with ill intent:

Why do you think telling the truth helps, causes, or enables us to become more like Christ?

What does God command us to do in verse 25?

How does telling lies ruin community?

We are to speak the truth in love to our neighbors and friends because it builds all of us up. It allows for freedom and community. If a community you are a part of is secretive and demands silence and cover up, you are not in a safe community. (Tomorrow we'll talk about safe people, and in the fourth week we'll talk about safe communities.)

Why don't we tell our secrets? Consider eight reasons:

1. The system (usually family but can be a ministry, church, group of friends, or school) prevents it. To expose the flaws or underbelly of that system invites wrath. The stakes are high because if you share, you risk losing every relationship within that system.

2. Shame can play a role, particularly if the secret has to do with sexual abuse or exploitation, or any other occurrence you'd rather not share. In the embrace of shame, it's easy to heap blame on yourself, or pull yourself up by your bootstraps (if you can) to pretend everything's okay—anything to prevent that story from coming to the light.

3. People want a happy world. So if you share a difficult story about their world (something bad happened in their circle), you shatter it. Better to keep it quiet to preserve their need for an all-is-well life.

4. There may be consequences (social, legal, societal) to sharing.

5. We may be experiencing "learned helplessness," a term coined by Dr. Martin Seligman.[1] This happens when we believe our actions or outcries mean nothing—that no matter what we do, we will never see improvement to our situation. This prevents us from speaking up because, what's the point? Nothing will ever change.

6. Some of us have experienced trauma, and the nature of trauma means many don't disclose for years. Why? Because in the moment of their painful story, they did not "fight back" or run from it. Instead, they froze. So somehow they think they're to blame for the pain.

7. Some don't tell secrets because of threats. People have threatened to sue, or terminate a job, or remove an inheritance. Some have experienced threats of violence or public shaming.

8. It's sometimes difficult to believe it was abuse, especially if the person abusing us had a position of power and control over us. With his or her blaming, gaslighting, and threats, we can believe his or her narratives over our own, not trusting our gut.

Do any of these reasons resonate with you? Explain.

Read Matthew 10:26-28.

What do these verses teach us about secrets?

How does that truth bring comfort? Does it scare you?

What is the command Jesus gives in verse 28?

When it comes to secrets, what does it mean to fear God (rather than fearing the opinion of others)?

Whether you suffered trauma at the hands of another human being or your trauma came into your life another way, consider the power of letting your story out. Think about someone's story, while it may or may not be like yours, that when brought to the light, encouraged or challenged you in your faith. When we share our stories, we testify to the power that humans cannot destroy us. By bringing our stories into the light, we prove we fear God above others.

DAY THREE
SAFE PEOPLE

When we dare to tell our stories, it's important the people receiving our stories are safe. When others tell us their stories, it's important we are safe. Sadly, most of us can recall a time when sharing our stories was not well received. Some threw clichés our way, laced with pulled-out-of-context Bible verses. Others tried to one-up our stories with their tale of woe. Others dismissed us. Even some called us liars. When people do this, it contributes to a secondary violation.

We know how painful it is to walk through someone's difficult response, and as empathetic followers of Jesus, we can choose to do better. We can become safe people.

In today's study we'll look at how to do just that, but we'll also explore the characteristics of safe folks. Why? Because when we entrust our hearts to another, it is a sacred trust.

Read Matthew 7:6.

What do you think Jesus meant when He told us not to throw pearls before pigs?

In the original context, Jesus' followers would have taken His words to refer to offering sacrificial meat to dogs or sacred teachings to pigs. We can see the danger in that—neither dogs nor pigs value these sacred things. In fact, it says that pigs may turn against the one bringing them pearls, symbolizing those who turn against not only the gospel, but also the messenger. Based on this context, we can see how these verses might relate to telling our own stories to others.

How does this verse tie into entrusting your story (that painful part of your narrative) to an unsafe person?

Of course, Jesus was the safest (in terms of relational kindness) person on earth. He exuded empathy. He listened. He healed the broken. He released those who had been possessed by demons. He told stories in order to help people live differently. He wept. He prayed. He pursued those who many dismissed.

He saved His harshest words for the hypocrites. Jesus confronted the religious elite for failing to love the people who had been entrusted to them.

Read Matthew 23.

How were the Pharisees unsafe (vv. 1-7)?

List the seven woes Jesus pronounced on these teachers of the law, according to these verses:

13-14:

15:

16-22:

23-24:

25-26:

27-28:

29-32:

We see the pastoral heart of Jesus in verses 37-39.

What did He lament in verse 37?

Why do you think Jesus wept over His children? Does He continue to weep over us today?

While the Pharisees exemplified unsafe people, throughout the New Testament, we see the qualities of safe people.

Read Galatians 5:22-26.

How does the fruit of the Holy Spirit make someone safe?

FRUIT	HOW DOES THAT MAKE SOMEONE SAFE?
Love	
Joy	
Peace	
Patience	
Kindness	
Goodness	
Faithfulness	
Gentleness	
Self-control	

Read 2 Peter 1:5-7.

List the seven things Peter instructs us to add to our faith.

How do these traits help make someone safe?

As we press in to Christ, as we seek Him with all our hearts and surrender our agendas and lives to Him, we inevitably become safer and safer because of the powerful work of the Holy Spirit. We are being transformed from glory to glory (2 Cor. 3:18) as we work out our salvation with fear and trembling (Phil. 2:12). The old is gone; the new awaits (2 Cor. 5:17). Our continued walk with Christ can't help but produce fruit like this, but sometimes it helps to see tangibly what a safe person acts like in the world. The following list is excerpted from my book *Not Marked: Finding Hope and Healing after Sexual Abuse*.

Safe people ...

- [ ] Ask clarifying questions.
- [ ] Don't jump to conclusions.
- [ ] Aren't passive-aggressive.
- [ ] Empathize with you, not needing to interject their own story of doom to one-up you.
- [ ] Encourage other relationships.
- [ ] Honor and encourage your relationship with God.
- [ ] Want the best for you and your healing journey (don't have their own healing agenda or pressure you to heal their way).
- [ ] Aren't domineering.
- [ ] Tell the truth—even the painful truth—but they tell it in a winsome way.
- [ ] Offer grace.
- [ ] Are self-aware.
- [ ] Reveal their flaws.
- [ ] Aren't defensive.
- [ ] Apologize, even before they're caught.
- [ ] Take responsibility for themselves.
- [ ] Work on their own issues.
- [ ] Want to learn from their mistakes.
- [ ] Accept blame.
- [ ] Avoid gossip.
- [ ] Are humble, teachable.
- [ ] Have a positive influence over your life.
- [ ] Have proven themselves trustworthy over a period of time.
- [ ] Are the same person in different situations—consistent.
- [ ] Applaud your growth.
- [ ] Don't try to parent you or act as the Holy Spirit.
- [ ] Love freedom.
- [ ] Don't demand trust—instead they earn it by consistently acting honorably.[2]

Look over this list. Put a star next to the traits you would like to see in yourself. Check those you need to work on. Think of a person whom you know as safe. Circle his or her traits.

How has your friend been a safe person to you?

Which of these qualities comes easily to you? Which do you need to work on in order to be a safe person for others to entrust their stories with?

It's important to note that even Christ followers can share unsafe traits. We all are on a journey toward health and compassion.

To end today's session, take some time to pray for the safe *and* unsafe people in your life. Ask Jesus to teach you to become more and more safe—someone people would turn to in a crisis.

DAY FOUR
LISTENING

If we want to be the hands and feet (and heart!) of Jesus to a broken world, there's a simple formula: Open ears + closed mouth = true empathy.

Many times, when someone approaches us with a difficult story, we panic, worrying we won't know what to say. But perhaps we should rest in knowing that people in pain are far more in need of our attentiveness rather than our advice.

I sat across from a new friend, a grandfather figure, who listened to a difficult part of my story I do not share in public. It was a risk, but I sensed he was safe. And he was. The moment the painful memory erupted from my story, his eyes teared up. For a long time, he said nothing, and in that space of silence, I felt utterly heard. He composed himself, then offered a few short sentences of empathy. Those words stayed with me, but even more than that, I remember the look on his face, the tears trailing down his cheek.

When I look at Jesus in the Gospel narratives, I imagine hundreds of people with a similar story. To them, Jesus was the empathetic listener, the validator of stories, the one who stopped His hectic life to listen and learn. He was never hurried. He often inconvenienced Himself for the sake of others.

Throughout Scripture we see the importance of guarding our tongues. Let's dive in to some of its instruction and cautionary tales.

> Take control of what I say, O Lord, and guard my lips.
> PSALM 141:3

Who can we turn to when we want to guard what we say?

What prevents you from asking God for help in the things you say?

Ecclesiastes 3:7 says there is "a time to be quiet and a time to speak." Can you recount a time in your life when you knew it was a time to be quiet?

When has God compelled you to speak up?

> Spouting off before listening to the facts
> is both shameful and foolish.
> **PROVERBS 18:13**

What happens when we reveal our opinions about a person before we've spent time understanding the whole situation?

Have you been the recipient of someone else "spouting off"?

Recount a time when you disobeyed this particular verse. What happened? What do you wish you would have done instead?

> Don't be selfish; don't try to impress others. Be humble, thinking of others as better than yourselves. Don't look out only for your own interests, but take an interest in others, too.
> **PHILIPPIANS 2:3-4**

When loving someone who is hurting, what does it look like to lay down your own selfishness and pay attention to his or her needs? What part does listening play in that endeavor?

Read James 1:19-26.

Verse 19 gives us one quick and two slows. What are they?

1. Quick to _____.

2. Slow to _____.

3. Slow to _____.

Why do you think James, the brother of Jesus, equated what we say with listening to God's Word?

What makes our religion worthless? Why do you think James used such strong language here?

What we say reveals our hearts, and it is a great barometer for how well we love the people in our lives.

Read James 3:1-12.

James used six metaphors when he referred to the tongue. Unpack them below.

METAPHOR	HOW THE TONGUE IS SIMILAR TO OR DIFFERENT FROM THE METAPHOR
Horse bit	
Ship rudder	
Fire	
Animals	
Spring	
Tree	

Read 1 John 2:9-11.

List the similarities in this passage and James 3:9.

If we claim we love God, we must demonstrate that same love toward those made in His image. To tear apart another with our words is an anathema to the gospel.

What does this have to do with helping others? Everything. Let's turn back to the Old Testament and unpack what happened to Job. Initially, his friends offered solace and deep comfort. Look at how they responded to his devastating losses in Job 2:11-13:

> When three of Job's friends heard of the tragedy he had suffered, they got together and traveled from their homes to comfort and console him. Their names were Eliphaz the Temanite, Bildad the Shuhite, and Zophar the Naamathite. When they saw Job from a distance, they scarcely recognized him. Wailing loudly, they tore their robes and threw dust into the air over their heads to show their grief. Then they sat on the ground with him for seven days and nights. No one said a word to Job, for they saw that his suffering was too great for words.

Have you ever felt like your suffering was "too great for words"? Describe the feeling.

How do you think Job felt as his friends demonstrated their care for him in this passage?

Things began well, but Job's friends did not continue or finish well. Clichéd sentiments, passive-aggressive judgments, and downright blame make up the bulk of the Book of Job.

Read God's indictment of Job's friends in Job 42:7-17.

What was God's accusation against Job's friends (v. 8)?

What did Job do prior to God restoring his fortunes? What does that say to us about the importance of praying for those who have hurt us?

To become someone who others come to for comfort, we must realize the power of our tongues. It seems an impossible task. It's difficult to listen, especially when we want to share our opinions. Thankfully, we have an Advocate in the Holy Spirit who intercedes for us when we slip up in this area. He empowers us to be silent when necessary. He helps us find encouraging words in the midst of crisis. We don't need to worry about what we will say—He is gracious to provide.

Rest in that promise today.

DAY FIVE
EMPATHY

When Jesus walked this earth, He had an air of irresistibility about Him. People could not help but flock to Him. Often, He had to escape crowds of people longing to be near Him. Little children climbed up on His lap—anyone who observes children knows they don't clamor to be in an adult's presence unless that person is sweet-tempered and approachable.

To be like Jesus is to demonstrate His empathy toward those who hurt. It's to place yourself in their situation, trying to see things from their perspective. So many of today's great societal ills could be resolved simply through the power of trying to understand what someone else's life must be like.

Jesus, as God incarnate, left the pristine beauty of heaven to ultimately (and completely) empathize with humankind. He walked the dusty pathways of Galilee. He bled. He went hungry. He worked with His hands. He experienced temptation and heartache. He felt the weight of grief and loss. He endured hardship, betrayal, and despair. All for us.

In writing that, I fall in love again with Jesus.

That's the hope of this study—not that you would embark on behavioral modification and try-try-try to listen more and demonstrate empathy, but that you would pursue the One who embodied that word.

We cannot do this kind of empathetic work for others in our own strength. We need the power of the Holy Spirit within us to produce this beautiful fruit.

> Take a moment right now to write out a prayer of surrender to Jesus. Ask Him to change your heart (only He can) and imbue you with empathy for those who are hurting. He loves to answer this kind of prayer.

The Book of Romans is the apostle Paul's love letter to the church in Rome. It's full of rich theology, cautionary tales, and exhortations on how we are to act in community. Romans 12 has a series of commands, but I want us to concentrate on a verse tucked into its belly, one we may miss as we read the entire chapter.

Read Romans 12:15.

While it's a joy to laugh with those who are happy, it takes an empathetic person to weep with those who weep. Why do you think Paul included this verse in the Romans 12 narrative? Why is it important to weep with those who cry out?

It seems pedestrian, doesn't it? Listen. Cry with those who cry. But sometimes it's the simple things that get overlooked. People are not looking for flash. They're not hankering after carefully scripted words. They want real. They want to feel heard. They want to know they're not alone. Empathy is the vehicle toward that simple end.

Let's read another one of Paul's treatises, this time looking at the word *comfort*.

Read 2 Corinthians 1:3-7.

Make six observations about the text, answering who, what, when, where, why, and how.

WHO	
WHAT	
WHEN	
WHERE	
WHY	
HOW	

The word for *comfort* here (in many forms) is ***paraklēseōs***. It means encouragement and comfort, but there are other important connotations.[3] Related to the word often used for the Holy Spirit (***paraklētos***), this hints at someone who comes alongside, who rushes to the aid of someone in peril.[4] It represents someone who is close beside you, someone who walks alongside in kindhearted assistance.

The New American Standard Bible reads, "God ... who comforts us in all our affliction so that we will be able to comfort those who are in any affliction with the comfort with which we ourselves are comforted by God" (vv. 3b-4).

What I love about this: God comforts us in all our afflictions. All. In every heartache, He comes alongside us, bearing our burdens, loving us through loss— every single one.

> What is the "so that" in verse 4? What does this imply we should do
> with the comfort we receive from God?

This comfort we receive qualifies us to help anyone in any affliction. Note that we don't have to have the same afflictions as the person we're bringing comfort to. God's comfort of us enables us to love people who have different stories of heartache.

Sometimes we think that in order to truly empathize, we have to have the exact same experience as the hurting person. While that does help empower empathy, we can still access God's comfort for someone who suffers differently.

For example, I have never experienced domestic violence. But I've walked with women who have. I have wept with them and sought to protect them. I could step into their heartache simply by remembering my own pain (though it differed), reminding myself of how God brought help.

My experience of God's comfort qualifies me to love those who suffer, regardless of whether I personally relate to the pain or not.

> When has someone been able to comfort you, or when have you been
> able to provide comfort based on God's comfort?

So in order to love people well, we have to avail ourselves to the comfort God readily gives us. That means we must pursue Him.

Some of you reading this, though, are angry with God. You don't believe He can be trusted. As you trace the narrative of your own story, you've asked, "Where were you, God, when I suffered?"

First, I am so sorry you've walked through your particular avenues of pain. I wish I could take those pathways away from you, and I understand how you feel. These kinds of questions are normal, and since God's heart for you is to be in relationship with Him, His desire is to interact with you about your questions and pain. After all, He already knows you have those feelings, so why not give them to Him?

I still have those questions, and the pain of them has somewhat subsided over the years. Living in a fallen world means that there will be people with free will who use that privilege to hurt others. On the other side of the veil, we will finally understand the whole story. Our tears will be gone, and justice will prevail. Right now, we see hazy. Someday, clarity will come.

I've come to the place where I echo Peter's words in John 6:68, "Lord, to whom would we go? You have the words that give eternal life."

He is the One who comforts, and if I run from Him, where will my comfort come from?

Have you ever asked the question, *Where were you, God?*

When has God brought comfort into your life?

We learn in 2 Corinthians 1:6 that our comfort, through the tutelage of the Holy Spirit, becomes a beautiful source of comfort for others. What we have endured is never for nothing. Our pain has purpose. It enables us to advocate for others.

I can honestly recount that some of the most profound moments of joy I've experienced in this life have been when I've had the privilege to pray for, support, and love someone in crisis. I felt alive, like I was actively part of expanding God's glorious kingdom. All of a sudden, all of that pain I endured made sense to me. Why? Because God redeemed my pain. He took me, a broken person, and remade me whole—whole enough to help those who struggle.

That is the power of the gospel in action, to be comforted so we can exercise empathy toward those who hurt. What a privilege!

THIS WEEK'S WE TOO MOMENT

Write a few sentences of gratitude to someone who has exemplified this week's study. Send it to them however you want (letter, email, text message, etc.).

- Who has welcomed your story?
- Who has held your secrets and offered solace?
- Who has been a safe person?
- Who has been an incredible listener?
- Who has demonstrated the empathy of Jesus to you?

Express your gratitude. Here's an example:

> *Leslie, I can't thank you enough for your prayer last night. It deeply encouraged me. It's like you knew that I had these doubts and struggles—like you really knew my heart—and you dared to pray for release and help. I so appreciate you. You truly are one of the most empathetic people I know, and I'm both humbled and grateful to call you friend.*

(Disclosure: I actually sent this just now!)

TRAUMA

Trauma is the painful gift that keeps on giving. Dr. Diane Langberg calls it "the mission field of our time."[1] It's absolutely necessary to understand and discern the nature of trauma in order to love people well (as well as unpack our own stories). So what is trauma?

In terms of our emotional and spiritual health, *Merriam-Webster* defines trauma as "a disordered psychic or behavioral state resulting from severe mental or emotional stress or physical injury."[2]

Trauma's effects are even more pronounced if you experienced it as a child. If you experienced divorce, parental death, sexual abuse, abandonment, emotional abuse, frequent moving, mental illness, an imprisoned parent, a severe accident, a life-threatening illness, poverty, violence in the home, parental drug abuse, or any life-altering event (particularly if you don't have a caring adult there to help you navigate it), you are more apt to battle heart disease, stroke, suicidal ideation, diabetes, or addiction later in life.[3]

Those who have had significant trauma also battle issues like:

- Depression
- Anxiety
- Panic attacks
- Hopelessness
- Belief in alienation (feeling like an outcast)
- Substance abuse
- Addictive behaviors such as watching porn, gambling, shopping, binging, and fasting
- Choice of friends or partners who abuse
- Low self-worth

Sadly, many who suffer these aftereffects sit in our pews, blaming themselves for their "inability" to get over their past. They believe they're fundamentally flawed, and that life will never improve. As I mentioned earlier, Martin Seligman calls this "learned helplessness."[4] When life beats you down again and again, you begin to believe that nothing you do will ever change things.

Thankfully (amazingly!), there is hope.

Trauma may have forced itself into your life or into the lives of your family and friends, but it does not have the final word. The final word was uttered by Jesus on the cross. "He said, 'It is finished,'" (John 19:30, ESV). The reign of sin (yes, even the sin enacted against you) has been cut short. The specter of death has been eradicated. And with the gift of the Holy Spirit within us, we have an Advocate who loves us, intercedes for us, and walks with us as we navigate life in the aftermath of pain.

This does not mean we don't avail ourselves to great resources like trauma therapy, retreats, or medication, but it does mean that even in the darkest pit, we have One who will never leave us or forsake us.

God beckons us toward *shalom*—a Hebrew term that encompasses far more than "peace from war."[5] *Shalom* is whole health—mind, soul, body, and spirit. God desires our wellness, and He has given us many stories to learn from in the biblical narrative that will empower us toward that end. Let's explore those together.

Mind if I pray for you?

*Jesus, for those who have experienced trauma, I pray for **shalom**. For those who are walking others through trauma, bring insight, kindness, and patience. Help us to understand the journeys others have walked, even though we may not have the same story. Renew our hope. Help us to battle cynicism and embrace forgiveness today. Amen.*

VIEWER GUIDE
SESSION THREE

What encouraged you about the video teaching this week?

Why do you think it's helpful to tell your story, to bring it into the light?

How have you seen God take an "I was" statement and change it into "I am" and "I will" statements, either in your own life or in the life of someone you know?

How can you encourage a friend stuck in the "I was"?

Teaching sessions available for purchase or rent at LifeWay.com/IntoTheLight

DAY ONE
HOW NOT TO RESPOND

Like we talked about in the first session of this study, the Bible often tells stories of trauma and sin. The inclusion of such stories in the pages of Scripture does not signal to us that God approves of the behavior in those stories. They are often simply descriptions of what life is like in our fallen, broken world.

Case in point, the story of Tamar in 2 Samuel 13. This is more a cautionary tale than a how-to story.

Read 2 Samuel 13.

Make six observations about the text, answering who, what, when, where, why, and how.

WHO	
WHAT	
WHEN	
WHERE	
WHY	
HOW	

What was your first response in reading this story today?

What surprised you about the story? Did anything cause anger? Explain your thoughts.

Note Tamar's very clear protests—how she said no: "No, my brother!" she said to him. "Don't force me! Such a thing should not be done in Israel! Don't do this wicked thing" (13:12, NIV).

Tamar pleaded with Amnon, to no avail. "But he refused to listen to her, and since he was stronger than she, he raped her" (13:14, NIV).

This is clearly rape—an egregious, evil violation. He tricked; he forced; she said no; he overpowered and then raped.

But then Amnon switched gears. He despised her and asked his servant to lock her out of his room. Tamar's response is poignant and comprehensible to anyone who has experienced such violation:

> She was wearing an ornate robe, for this was the kind of garment the virgin daughters of the king wore. Tamar put ashes on her head and tore the ornate robe she was wearing. She put her hands on her head and went away, weeping aloud as she went. Her brother Absalom said to her, "Has that Amnon, your brother, been with you? Be quiet for now, my sister; he is your brother. Don't take this thing to heart." And Tamar lived in her brother Absalom's house, a desolate woman.
> **2 SAMUEL 13:18b-20 (NIV)**

The transliteration of the word desolate here is *wašōmêmāh*. It is the only time this particular form of the word is used in the Old Testament. It means devastated, desecrated (as in desecrating a sanctuary), ruined, deserted, laid waste, and forsaken.[6]

Have you ever experienced feelings of desolation like this?

Devastated, desecrated, ruined, deserted, laid waste, forsaken—does this describe someone in your life? If so, how have you come alongside him or her?

Later, Absalom avenged Tamar's rape, but his response in the moment after the violation serves to remind us of modern-day responses to trauma.

- Be quiet.
- He is your brother (pastor, teacher, boyfriend, husband).
- Don't take this thing to heart.

Clearly, Tamar withered under this callous, non-empathetic advice. She lived out her years desolate. Once a girl with promise, the king's daughter, she became a sequestered exile who lived without hope.

Sadly, when we tell traumatized people to be quiet, then to submit to silence for the sake of the reputation of the one who enacted that trauma, all while encouraging them not to take things to heart, the survivor withers as well.

Shame flourishes in silence. And in the case of Tamar, it stole her future. No longer a virgin, she was not marriageble. The narrative, thankfully, reveals the abject desperation of Tamar and the obvious, sinful predation of her half-brother—it does not sugarcoat. But that honesty doesn't take away the very real consequences of the perpetrator's actions.[7]

> Looking at the story of Tamar as a cautionary tale, how should we not respond to someone who has been traumatized?

> Observe what you wrote. Write an opposite statement for each example you wrote (shut her down versus listen, for example). This will reflect what we should do when we encounter a devastated person.

Not everyone we cross paths with will have a similar story to Tamar's, but we can still take direction from this story.

We can understand the very real power of empathy. We can welcome stories. If a crime has been committed, we can report it instead of handling it "in house." We can realize the longevity of the pain, how it affects someone for a lifetime. This will prevent us from slapping clichéd statements on an open wound.

As discussed last week, we can learn from the stories of the Tamars of the world, feeling their pain and looking at their difficult situations with a new, informed perspective.

DAY TWO
HOW TO RESPOND

It's not always easy to learn from negative examples. Sometimes we need to see compassion demonstrated. Actions are powerful, and we have a poignant example of those kinds of redemptive acts in the story of Naomi and Ruth.

In Ruth, we see an empathetic doer. Her words and actions matched up. And in her bravery as an outsider to the nation of Israel, she preserved a family line, brought healing to a brokenhearted woman, and lived to see redemption in tangible, beautiful ways.

Let's watch her in action.

Read Ruth 1.

Make six observations about the text, answering who, what, when, where, why, and how.

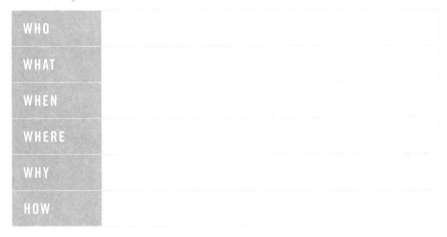

WHO	
WHAT	
WHEN	
WHERE	
WHY	
HOW	

We see much trauma and desolation in this story right at the onset.

A famine exiled Naomi's family to Moab. Her husband and two sons died, leaving her alone with her sons' two Moabite wives, Orpah and Ruth, who vowed to accompany her back to Judah.

Naomi told them not to bother, then said, "Things are far more bitter for me than for you, because the LORD himself has raised his fist against me" (v. 13b).

Yet Ruth persisted and then accompanied her mother-in-law back to Judah. She revealed her tenacious kindness with love backed by action.

Ruth famously said, "Don't ask me to leave you and turn back. Wherever you go, I will go; wherever you live, I will live. Your people will be my people, and your God will be my God. Wherever you die, I will die, and there I will be buried. May the LORD punish me severely if I allow anything but death to separate us!" (vv. 16-17).

What did Ruth promise Naomi in this declaration?

How does her reaction demonstrate the *hesed* (the loyal, covenantal love) of God?[8]

How is Ruth similar to the Holy Spirit, in terms of the role He plays in our lives now?

Reread Ruth 1:20-21.

What did Naomi call herself?

Mara in Hebrew means "bitter" or "embittered."[9] Naomi's life was typified by depression and deep sadness.

Have you ever felt that way? What circumstances brought you to a place of brokenness?

In the remainder of the book of Ruth, we see Ruth continued to love Naomi in tangible ways. She gleaned Boaz's fields and brought back provision. This certainly was a risk as a single widowed woman. She, too, was a foreigner, not privy to the rights of Judean citizens. But her love for Naomi, the bitter one, continued.

We learn that Boaz had the potential to be a kinsman redeemer—one who is related to Naomi and could provide for them in this desperate situation. Through a series of interesting antics (Ruth laying at Boaz's feet and Boaz bargaining with another kinsman so he can become the kinsman redeemer of Naomi's family), Boaz was free to marry Ruth, enabling Naomi to have an heir. Her entire narrative changed, from bitter to fruitful, from empty to embraced, from desperate to blessed—all because of Ruth's ardent devotion to her and her God.

What characteristics of Ruth gave hope to Naomi?

What does it mean to be a Ruth today?

Read Ruth 4:13-17.

List the amazing, positive things that happened to Naomi at the end of this book.

Who, do we learn, is David's grandfather? Why is that significant?

Isn't it amazing that one woman's kindhearted words and actions in the face of trauma changed not only the course of a nation, but ushered in the lineage of Jesus Christ? There is power in responding well to those in crisis.

> Think about who you know that might be going through a crisis or responding to trauma. How can you be like Ruth in his or her life—encouraging, offering sympathy, and helping point him or her to Christ?

DAY THREE
TRAUMA CREATORS

Predatory people exist. We certainly see evidence in the Tamar narrative from day one of this week's study. Predatory people can exist within our families, churches, seminaries, schools, and missions organizations. A high percentage of our trauma comes from a predatory person or people harming us. Therefore, it's important we understand their natures. We must discern who they are and how to respond in the aftermath of their actions.

A common misconception is that people who harm others look or act a certain way. They drive around in windowless vans, neglect personal hygiene, or stand out as awkward in a crowd. But the truth is, most predatory people seem kind. Consider this quote about Larry Nassar, the USA gymnastics doctor who perpetrated against hundreds of young girls.

"[Larry Nassar] was up early and went to bed late. He would do anything for an injured athlete. He was an astonishingly giving person."[10]

Niceness, we have come to learn, is not a character trait. It is a learned behavior. This is part of a perpetrator's DNA—become excessively nice, outgoing, charming, and helpful. That way, when he or she is exposed, most people will be utterly shocked. Surely that nice man or woman didn't do those horrible things. There must be a mistake!

I remember when my husband and I were church planters in France. Up until that time, I had taken note of the New Testament warnings of wolves in sheep's clothing (Matt. 7:15) but naively believed they were written for back then, not today. But we ended up encountering several wolves in Christian clothing, using Christian language, yet acting in a completely different way.

It's imperative we understand this problem. Why? Because perhaps the most difficult relational trauma to overcome is that which happens under the guise of Christianity. We can rationalize why a non-believer would act unbecomingly, but a believer? Why would they do that? Shouldn't they have treated us with respect?

We are seeing an exodus in the church precisely because of this unspoken issue.

   Read 2 Corinthians 11:13-15.

What does it mean that Satan "disguises himself as an angel of light" (v. 14)? Why do you think he does that? How does doing that tear down the church?

According to Ephesians 6:12, who is our daily battle against?

Read Matthew 10:16.

How do we accomplish this in our daily lives?

Why do you think Jesus gave us this command? Why was it necessary?

We must be wise about those who harm, yes, but we must also be alert to the ways we harm others. Asking Jesus to search our hearts, having safe friends who tell us the truth, and possessing a love for Scripture and adherence to prayer, we can begin to understand our own tendency toward harm.

That's why our own healing journey is important. If we shove down our pain and don't let it out in the light of day, we may end up repeating the very things we vowed we'd never do. Our hurt hearts reveal themselves in actions.

As I mentioned earlier, your best gift to your loved ones is a healed heart. It's making a decision to do life differently. It's placing a holy marker in the ground and saying, "No more on my watch."

As you begin to heal, your understanding of how another person's predatory actions have affected you will blossom. You'll begin to uncover patterns. You'll soon realize when you have reverted back to that which you knew and experienced. Sadly, our comfortable place is often a dysfunctional one. To grow is to forsake that which feels normal. So moving forward not only prevents you from becoming predatory toward others, but it also sets your feet on new ground, in that scary place where faith to grow is necessary.

Read 2 Corinthians 5:17.

How does this promise encourage you today?

As Christ followers, we are walking a brand new journey. Though predatory people exist, and they have brought hurt into our lives and the lives of others, sometimes our hearts prey on us. We can be our own worst bullies. Part of spiritual growth is learning to identify when we're self-shaming and condemning ourselves. Paul talked about this when he quoted Isaiah: "Everyone who believes in him will not be put to shame" (Rom. 10:11, ESV). Part of loving others is helping them recognize when they are bullying themselves.

Read 1 John 3:18-22.

In loving those who have been hurt by others, in what two ways does John encourage us to demonstrate love toward those who have been hurt by others?

How do you know that you belong to the truth?

Have you ever battled a hyperactive conscience? (Example: You apologized for something you didn't do wrong, just in case.) If so, how have you battled it this week?

What does verse 20 remind us about God's ability to love and care for us?

Do our feelings of condemnation negate the bedrock reality of God's love?

What does it mean in your life to have confidence before God? Do you struggle to have this? Why or why not?

We learn freedom in the promises of these verses. God is bigger than our own self-bullying ways. Because of Jesus and His life, death, and resurrection, we are given entrance into a new kingdom. The old has gone. The new erupts! In light of that, we can endure and overcome trauma and hurt in our lives. We can learn the art of letting go of the critical self inside us. (This is not the same as conviction of sin, but a pervasive feeling of shame.) And we can begin to understand the pain of others.

Looking back on the story of Ruth, we can see the power of someone who rescues people who are in precarious and dangerous situations, who are vulnerable to be preyed upon. Boaz did just that for Ruth and Naomi. And through the power of the Holy Spirit, we can do the same for others.

DAY FOUR
PRAYER

In college, I was deeply broken. I overshared. I cried a lot. The trauma from my past roared to life once I was in a safe place to fall apart. And in that messiness, I asked for prayer. I needed it. I sought it. God changed me through the prayers of other kindhearted people.

Prayer is the air we breathe. It's our ongoing communication with God throughout the day. I believe every single Christian needs prayer in his or her healing journey. Why? Because we need God's supernatural power to overcome what tried to overcome us.

When we minister to other broken people, prayer is vital too. We need the intersection of God and our stories, and prayer is a perfect way to experience that.

I have a podcast called *Pray Every Day*, where I pray for people all over the world according to Scripture. I read a few verses and then pray about the content of those verses. It's been such a privilege to do so, and I've had the joy of receiving emails from people who live in other countries sharing how this simple act has helped them move closer to healing.

Today, we're going to pause a moment and study this important privilege, exploring what kind of role prayer has as we minister to those who are hurting.

Did you know that the Lord's Prayer provides a pattern for growth in relationships? That is the premise of my book *The Wall Around Your Heart*. In it, I walk readers through every phrase of the prayer as a way to heal from broken relationships. We have recited the prayer so often I fear we have lost the rich advice and practice it promotes.

Read Matthew 6:9-13 and Luke 11:2-4.

> Our Father in heaven,
> hallowed be your name.
> **MATTHEW 6:9b (ESV)**

What do you think it means that Jesus used the word "our" in "our Father" (instead of "my")?

How do we hallow (praise, honor) God with our lives?

How can hallowing God with our lives affect the way we treat others?

> Your kingdom come,
> your will be done,
> on earth as it is in heaven.
> **MATTHEW 6:10 (ESV)**

Think of your most difficult relationship currently. What would it look like to see God's kingdom come in the midst of that relationship?

Consider someone who's hurting. Dream about what his or her healed life may look like. What comes to mind?

Sometimes, when we help others, we accidentally replace God for them. They turn to us rather than Him. Once when I did that with a close friend (calling her before I called out to God), she told me, "I make a poor Jesus." And she was right. If we are people's saviors, we will sadly disappoint them. But if we understand our role as followers who point people to Jesus, we will empower them to find their solace in Him.

> Give us this day our daily bread.
> **MATTHEW 6:11 (ESV)**

Why is it important to point people to the daily provision of God?

When have you tried to be your own provision? Or the sole provision
for someone else? How did that turn out?

And forgive us our debts,
as we also have forgiven our debtors.
MATTHEW 6:12 (ESV)

So many of us have tried to understand forgiveness. Is it a one-time occurrence?
Is it layered and a long journey? How does that relate to prayer? One thing
traumatized people have endured is helpers telling them (demanding) to
forgive on their timetable. We must be careful not to prescribe someone else's
forgiveness journey. The Spirit directs that part of our stories.

To forgive is to understand Jesus' amazing forgiveness of us. It allows for the
possibility of reconciliation, but it cannot guarantee it. Forgiveness provides the
atmosphere for a renewed relationship, but to truly experience reconciliation,
both parties must want to. You cannot force someone to reconcile with you, even
if you have forgiven.

When we shoulder the weight of people's pain, it's imperative we be sensitive to
the Spirit's leading in their lives. Let them bring up the topic of their forgiveness
journey. Ask questions. Agree with them as they pray forgiveness prayers—but
don't mandate.

Have you had the opportunity to pray with someone who is choosing
to forgive someone who hurt him or her? Have you chosen to forgive,
then prayed in the presence of someone else about it, or was it
a private act? What happened?

And lead us not into temptation,
but deliver us from evil.
MATTHEW 6:13 (ESV)

What is your primary temptation when someone has deeply wounded you?

Jesus ended His prayer by asking for deliverance from evil. In the Tamar story, note that at no point did any of the predatory people or bystanders seek God. They simply participated or allowed the evil to proceed, unchecked.

But our mandate is different. One of the most powerful things we can do in prayer and in the midst of honest relationship is to acknowledge the evil someone has endured. To deny it is to rob someone of his or her story. But to enter into it, calling evil what it is, you invite someone to community. Suddenly, he or she feels understood, loved, and listened to.

As we pray for others, we must remember that the act of prayer is spiritual warfare, pulling down strongholds, exposing lies, and inviting God's supernatural power into a situation. That's why prayer is so important. In essence it says:

- I can't.
- God can.
- Help!

When someone is facing a difficult situation, and his or her problems feel insurmountable, Jonah's prayer is helpful.

Read Jonah 2.

Make six observations about the text, answering who, what, when, where, why, and how.

WHO	
WHAT	
WHEN	
WHERE	
WHY	
HOW	

According to the Book of Jonah, God answered his prayer for deliverance. (The fact that his prayer is recorded attests to this; otherwise, it would have been swallowed by the big fish!)

Think of a hurting friend or family member. Below are the six actions God does on behalf of Jonah. In the chart below, answer how this truth encourages you today, and how it can encourage that hurting person.

TRAIT/ACTION OF GOD	HOW IT ENCOURAGES YOU	HOW IT CAN ENCOURAGE A HURTING PERSON
He is a shield.		
He is our glory.		
He lifts my head.		
He answers us.		
He sustains us.		
He delivers us.		

An oft-forgotten form of prayer that is entirely necessary in the healing journey is praise. When we learn to praise God, we transform our thinking from pain toward gratitude. Hannah is an excellent example of a woman in pain who both prayed and praised.

Read 1 Samuel 2:1-10.

Then Hannah prayed:
"My heart rejoices in the LORD!
The LORD has made me strong.
Now I have an answer for my enemies;
I rejoice because you rescued me.
No one is holy like the LORD!
There is no one besides you;
there is no Rock like our God.
"Stop acting so proud and haughty!
Don't speak with such arrogance!
For the LORD is a God who knows what you have done;
he will judge your actions.
The bow of the mighty is now broken,
and those who stumbled are now strong.
Those who were well fed are now starving,
and those who were starving are now full.
The childless woman now has seven children,
and the woman with many children wastes away.
The LORD gives both death and life;
he brings some down to the grave but raises others up.
The LORD makes some poor and others rich;
he brings some down and lifts others up.
He lifts the poor from the dust
and the needy from the garbage dump.
He sets them among princes,
placing them in seats of honor.
For all the earth is the LORD's,
and he has set the world in order.
"He will protect his faithful ones,
but the wicked will disappear in darkness.
No one will succeed by strength alone.
Those who fight against the LORD will be shattered.
He thunders against them from heaven;
the LORD judges throughout the earth.
He gives power to his king;
he increases the strength of his anointed one."

Now do the following:
• Circle the times Hannah praised God.

• Underline God's actions.

• Put a box around God's traits.

• Put a squiggly line under painful circumstances.

What do you learn about God in this passage?

What do you learn about hurting people from Hannah's prayer?

How can learning to praise God and becoming content help us as we help others?

I would not be where I am today without people daring to pray for me. While we don't want to force prayer, we can lead the kind of invitational lives that open up spaces for us to pray for others. Some people may be so damaged by other Christians that prayer may be too scary for them. Respect their boundaries. Prayer, of course, is not limited to in-person petition only. We can battle for the broken on our knees privately too.

Take some time to pray for the people who came to your mind during today's study. Pray for healing, for hope, and that you might be a source of light for them.

DAY FIVE
WALKING ALONGSIDE

We perplex over why people stream out the back doors of our churches. Why do they leave? They leave in large part because we have not properly made discipleship the longing of the church, the great heartbeat of the gospel.

To disciple another is to walk alongside, to hear, to teach, to reproduce our faith in Jesus, infusing His love into the life of another. Discipleship is about relationship, connection, conversation, prayer, and powerful empathy. But if we dismiss the hurting, the broken, and the abused, we cease being the disciple-making church, and we instead become citadels of unreality and privilege. In short, we shirk the joyful responsibility it is to truly disciple everyday people.[11]

Jesus modeled discipleship for us in the Gospels by walking alongside the broken. He physically walked to many villages with His disciples, practicing peripatetic spirituality.

Peripateō is a commonly used Greek word in the New Testament with two basic meanings. One is to meander, to circumvent, to walk, or to go about. Jesus did a lot of this type of *peripateō* with His disciples. He walked dusty pathways. He climbed mountains with His followers. He ambled alongside. He spent time with them. He was present in each moment. I find it fascinating that Jesus didn't start His formal ministry on earth until He had first been present, rubbing shoulders with humankind for thirty years.

The second meaning of *peripateō* is the manner in which someone lives his or her life, the way he or she behaves.[12] The apostle Paul used this word a lot: "Therefore I, a prisoner for serving the Lord, beg you to lead a life worthy of your calling, for you have been called by God" (Eph. 4:1). "Dear brothers and sisters, pattern your lives after mine, and learn from those who follow our example" (Phil. 3:17). Being with broken people as well as showing them by example how Jesus wants us to live is an important element of walking alongside.

What does it look like to walk with someone who is hurting? Let's explore that today.

    Read Galatians 6:1-10.

If we notice another believer caught in sin, in what manner should we approach him or her?

According to verse two, what is our mandate as we love others who carry heavy burdens?

Why is it important to approach the people in our lives with a gentle attitude? How does that help make disciples?

How does comparing yourself to someone else (v. 4) render you ineffective in caring for someone else?

I appreciate Paul's words in verses 9-10, "So let's not get tired of doing what is good. At just the right time we will reap a harvest of blessing if we don't give up. Therefore, whenever we have the opportunity, we should do good to everyone—especially to those in the family of faith." He reveals the reality of compassion fatigue, that as we help others, we will be tempted to give up.

Persevering is hard. It takes guts, the Spirit within, and a tenacity to continue forward with someone.

Who in your life are you struggling to persevere alongside? Why? What makes it difficult to keep moving forward?

As I write this, I am praying for you—that you would lean on the Spirit to give you the grit necessary to bear another's burden.

But what happens when we cannot go forward? What do we do when a burden overpowers us? How are we to proceed?

First, we have to recognize we are limited. As human beings, we are not designed to be saviors of others. There is only one Savior, and He beautifully promises to carry each person's burdens. Sure, we lighten the loads of others, but eventually they will need to find solace in the arms of Jesus. The discipleship journey involves us introducing people to Jesus, so that they will learn to go to Him for everything.

Read Matthew 11:28-30.

Who did Jesus invite in this passage?

What did He promise?

When Jesus promises a yoke, we may shrink back. Isn't a yoke painful? Doesn't it mean we will suffer under its weight? No, because the yoke Jesus gives us is one He bears the full weight of. He does the primary pulling work, while we are to simply walk alongside. What a beautiful promise.

When have you longed to have soul rest? Are you in that place right now?

How does knowing Jesus is pulling the bulk of the load help your perspective?

We cannot give away what we do not have. We must have an experience with Jesus first before we seek to give Him away.

While it's important to mentor and disciple those who are hurting, we must also be realistic and wise. We may have prayed, born the weight of others, and gone to Jesus for sustenance and rest, yet still our loved one is struggling, making little or no progress, or maybe he or she is spiraling, and we feel lost as we try to help.

This is when we must avail ourselves to a variety of resources. Just like we would take someone having a heart attack to the hospital (rather than only praying and offering empathy), we must take people with deeper trauma issues to those trained to deal with them.

Thankfully, you are not without resources. I have compiled an extensive list of helpful websites, books, articles, professionals, and services on WeToo.org/Resources. It takes wisdom to discern when you need to consult outside help, and you may need to consult with a professional on behalf of your hurting friend or family member to know how to best refer him or her to a safe place.

There have been times when someone with a great amount of needs and/or trauma has overwhelmed me. In those cases, I have turned to safe friends (outside the circle of the one I am helping to avoid gossip) and asked their advice. Sometimes, in our desire to help others, and our need to be the kind of person who is approached by others for help, we become blind to our own situation. I have had to rely on good friends to tell me if I am enabling, or to let me know when a relationship is harming me (or I am harming another).

The truth? We heal better in community. We need each other—even as we help, particularly if our tendency is to rescue or over-help. Having safe friends who pour their lives into us helps us have double discernment—theirs and ours—as we seek to love the broken in our lives. This is the beauty and power of community.

THIS WEEK'S WE TOO MOMENT

Go through WeToo.org/Resources, writing down or compiling a list of resources that may be helpful for the people in your life. Connect with your church's website to see what they offer (support groups, counseling services, Stephen ministries, Celebrate Recovery, small groups, etc.). Place all these links in a document so you can continue to add to it. You never know—this may end up helping someone in a desperate situation. After all, it's far better to be proactive than reactive.

SAFE CHURCHES

The church should be the safest place for those who suffer, but, sadly, it sometimes isn't. People who are broken, bleeding, and traumatized long for havens. They look for shepherds to tenderly care for them. They need good Samaritans to inconvenience themselves for the sake of healing and hope.

To our detriment, we often believe the church to be a building full of self-possessed people who rarely struggle without an accompanying victory story.

But the church is simply this: a people called out, redeemed by Christ. We all have broken stories. However, our wrecked state is not something to retreat from but instead can be an impetus for coming to Jesus. In the church, no one is better than anybody else. Leaders are simply people who serve and equip the body of believers to serve as well. The hierarchy is a mutual subjugation beneath Jesus, the head of our endeavors.

The church, the ones who have been called, the mercifully forgiven, are the hands and feet of Jesus on this earth. We are not corrupted or enticed by political position. We are not enthralled with power or might but take delight in embracing the weak.

We understand we serve Jesus when we love those who are hurting. We find Jesus in the face of the traumatized. We hear His voice trumpeted by the frail. We taste God's goodness when we say grace over a meal with the humble. We sense Him with us when we serve those whose stories are shattered. The church is not a place of perfection. It is, and should be, a haven of protection.[1]

You may have a story of pain related to how people within a church or its leaders have hurt you. Hurt from a church is one of the most painful injuries a heart has to endure. Why? Because we let our masks down when we interact with fellow believers. We trust them to act kindly. We have certain expectations of people who name the name of Christ or work in His service.

Sometimes we can equate the behavior of Christians to the character of God Himself. Why would someone in His name act unbecomingly? Being hurt by the church can, then, usher in a crisis of faith. Why follow a God whose followers are heartless?

I don't write that to impugn the entirety of the church. I realize I have the same capabilities to hurt other people, and I grieve over the times I have. The truth is, while I would like to believe the narrative that all the "bad" people are others, and I am the victim-hero, I have to realize that sin touches one hundred percent of humankind, infecting all of us with the capability to hurt others.

Some people who need our empathetic help come from this perspective of being marginalized by the church. The place that should provide healing has morphed into a judgmental, pain-inducing fiasco. In cases like these, we dance the difficult line between agreeing with the offense yet still loving Christ's body, the church.

This week we are going to take a hard look at the church—what it is and what a safe church looks like. We'll look at abuses with a discerning eye, while striving to understand the church's beauty.

Mind if I pray for you?

Jesus, I pray You would uncover places in hearts hurt by people in the church, not for continual introspection, but with a view toward redemption, healing, and moving gloriously forward. Be as near us as breath. Empower us with Your empathy for those who are hurting, and give discernment as we worship You among Your people. Amen.

VIEWER GUIDE
SESSION FOUR

What does it mean to assume positive intent? How can you do that with those around you, both in your home and in your community?

Have you ever built up a wall to prevent harm in your life? How did it work? What joy did you miss out on because of that wall?

Mary said the best gift you can give those you love is a healed heart. How does your healing affect those around you?

How can you become a safer person for someone else?

Teaching sessions available for purchase or rent at LifeWay.com/IntoTheLight

ANATOMY OF A GREAT CHURCH

There is no perfect church.

I have had to repeat this to myself over the years because I have never encountered one. By and large, each church operates like a family—supporting, conniving, redeeming, hiding—sometimes a place of condemning, other times a haven of rest.

Why is this so?

Because the body of Christ is made up of human beings, and we are tainted by sin. Yes, of course, those who have met Jesus have been set free from their old nature. Sin no longer holds its same sway over us, and we have been delivered from darkness to marvelous light, but that does not mean once we surrender to Jesus that our sin nature is totally eradicated. All of us are working out our "salvation with fear and trembling" (Phil. 2:12, ESV). All of us are on a journey. All of us are trying to understand how to love each other.

So many of us have difficult stories. We have been broken by life, health issues, disasters, and painful relationships. Those stories, if left unattended, can fester into new coping patterns that butt up against other people with difficult stories, causing friction and pain. As I mentioned earlier, the best gift to others is our own pursuit of healing. We have some modicum of control over our own healing, but as much as we might want and try to, we cannot make others heal. So the friction continues.

This pain has happened for millennia, even before the dawn of the church. Leaders struggled to love their people well. The nation of Israel faced exile for many reasons, one of which was the Israelites' neglect of the hurting in their midst.

Read Isaiah 58:1-7.

The message in this passage is from God, spoken by the prophet Isaiah. What is the primary thing God had against the leaders of Israel in this passage?

What does God require as a compassionate response to those hurting according to verses 6-7?

How can we apply this passage about ancient Israel to our churches today? How can we apply it to our own lives and faith?

Now let's look at the church in its embryonic stage, prior to Paul's conversion, when the Holy Spirit poured over the very first congregation. We will see a beautiful fulfillment of the Isaiah passage above, right down to tangible help given to those in need.

Read Acts 2:1-12,41-47.

Make six observations about the text, answering who, what, when, where, why, and how.

WHO

WHAT

WHEN

WHERE

WHY

HOW

The word "amazed" is used in describing Pentecost. What must it have been like to hear the praises of God in your own dialect when you most likely hadn't heard such a thing before? This birthing of the church began with the miracle of speech, then continued with a powerful oration by Peter—the very one who only a few months earlier had cowered when a servant girl asked him about his affiliation with Jesus (John 18:15-18). Something supernatural had obviously taken place.

When we read this passage, we remember the power of God. Seeking to help others can seem like an impossible task. When we try to work through our own stories, we may see a looming mountain whose pass seems insurmountable. But the truth is, God is big. He is powerful. His purposes prevail. He can do anything. He can utterly change a life.

In this account, three thousand people were transformed in a moment.

Reread Acts 2:42-47.

What did this embryonic church devote itself to?

How do we see these same things happen in church life today?

Why do you think miracles, signs, and wonders were displayed during this time?

I've often heard that the wallet of a believer is the last thing to be saved. How did these new believers demonstrate their kindness toward each other? How did they view their possessions and finances?

This community gathered. They loved each other. Why would that have been unusual or infectious?

We see an incredible parallel in Acts 4, revealing the consistency of the early church to share, see God do the miraculous, and sacrifice for each other.

Read Acts 4:32-37.

What are some similarities between what you read in Acts 2 and this passage?

How does the modern church resemble this early congregation? How does it differ?

God blesses us when we choose to radically love those in our midst. Let's return to Isaiah 58.

Read Isaiah 58:8-12 below.

> Then your light will break out like the dawn,
> And your recovery will speedily spring forth;
> And your righteousness will go before you;
> The glory of the Lord will be your rear guard.
> Then you will call, and the Lord will answer;
> You will cry, and He will say, "Here I am."
> If you remove the yoke from your midst,
> The pointing of the finger and speaking wickedness,
> And if you give yourself to the hungry
> And satisfy the desire of the afflicted,
> Then your light will rise in darkness
> And your gloom will become like midday.
> And the Lord will continually guide you,
> And satisfy your desire in scorched places,
> And give strength to your bones;
> And you will be like a watered garden,
> And like a spring of water whose waters do not fail.
> Those from among you will rebuild the ancient ruins;
> You will raise up the age-old foundations;
> And you will be called the repairer of the breach,
> The restorer of the streets in which to dwell (NASB).

As you look over that passage:

• Underline the promises of God you find in those verses.

• Circle the actions God requires of us.

It's compelling to see how the New Testament church acted in this same manner and how the promises of God were fulfilled. Light, recovery, satisfaction, guidance, strength, refreshment, rebuilding—all these typify a healthy, God-fearing congregation.

As we close today's study, spend some time thanking God for the healthy, God-fearing body of believers you call home. If you do not have such a place of refuge, pray now that God would help you find a safe, healthy church.

DAY TWO
SPIRITUAL ABUSE AND UNSAFE PLACES

Sometimes church can be a safe haven, a place of light and healing. I pray it has been for you. We know, though, that people sometimes find themselves in unhealthy, unsafe places of worship. And we also know that, sadly, sometimes ministries and churches perpetuate spiritual abuse.

I once wrote about unsafe places on my blog. I've included some of the post below. As you read, please keep in mind that every situation of trauma and abuse is different. It's always important to seek out wise counsel to help you discern next steps.

Often you don't realize you're in an abusive situation until your health is damaged, your soul is torn, or your outside relationships suffer, and you usually only discern this in retrospect. My heart in sharing this is to simply shed light on unhealthy, manipulative, controlling practices.

Spiritually abusive and unsafe ministries ...

- **Have a distorted view of respect.** They forget the simple adage that respect is earned, not granted. Abusive leaders demand respect without having earned it by good, honest living. They also demand allegiance as proof of the follower's allegiance to Christ. It's either his or her way or no way. And if a follower deviates, he or she is guilty of deviating from Jesus.

- **Use exclusive language.** "We're the only ministry really following Jesus." "We have all the right theology." Believe their way of doing things, thinking theologically or handling ministry and church, is the only correct way. Everyone else is wrong, misguided, or stupidly naive. In addition, followers close to the leader(s) feel like lucky insiders; everyone else is on the outside. If someone on the inner circle speaks up about abuses, lapses in character, illegal acts, or strong-arming, that insider immediately moves to an outsider. Fear of losing their special status often impedes insiders from speaking up.

- **Create a culture of fear and shame.** Often there is no grace for someone who fails to live up to the church's or ministry's expectations. And if someone steps outside of the often-unspoken rules, leaders shame them into compliance. Leaders can't admit failure but often search out failure in others and use that knowledge to hold them in fear and captivity. They often quote Scriptures about not touching God's anointed, or bringing accusations against an elder. Yet they often confront sin in others, particularly ones who bring up legitimate biblical issues. Or they have their circle of influence take on this task, silencing critics.

- **Demand blind servitude of their followers but live prestigious, privileged lives.** Where a leader might begin ministry interested in others' issues, he or she eventually withdraws to a small group of "yes people" and isolates from the needs of others. They buffer themselves from criticism by placing people around themselves whose only allegiance is to the leader.

- **Cultivate a dependence on one leader or leaders for spiritual information.** Personal discipleship isn't encouraged. Often the Bible gets pushed away to the fringes unless the main leader is teaching it. These leaders harbor a cult of personality, meaning if the central figure of the ministry or church left, the entity would collapse, as it was entirely dependent on one person to hold the place together.

- **Hold to outward performance but reject authentic spirituality.** Places burdens on followers to act a certain way, dress an acceptable way, and have an acceptable lifestyle, but they often demonstrate licentiousness, greed, and uncontrolled addictions behind closed doors. They live aloof from their followers and justify their material extravagance as God's favor and approval on their ministry. They typically chase after wealth—at any cost and often at the expense of the very people they shepherd.[2]

While these traits are painful, and for some reading this, eye-opening, it helps us to see the intent and hope of Jesus in how churches, ministries, and leaders should be instead. Let's look at that today.

Read Psalm 23.

What are qualities of the Lord in this passage? In other words, what does a shepherd do?

When you read this passage, how did you feel? What do you think God is saying to you today about your life?

Now read John 10:1-18.

According to this passage, what does a good shepherd do?

So what happens if you encounter a person or ministry that does not exemplify the Good Shepherd? Here are some thoughts.

Take your commitment seriously.

So many times we take the convenient way out. If someone hurts us, we are easily offended and don't want to take the time to work through the issues in a healthy manner. God calls us all to our local body of believers, and our covenant with those people (who are sinful just like us) is a serious, important one. We should not take lightly a desire to abandon the fellowship God has brought us to. (Of course it's different if you're dealing with a parachurch ministry, which is not the same thing as a local church body). In either case, it's wise to seek counsel and pray, asking God what He wants you to do in the midst of this painful situation.

Ask God if it's time to confront.

Read Matthew 18:15-17.

How does Jesus instruct us to confront those within the church?

This passage delineates when we should do this and the manner in which we should. If we've been hurt by someone, Jesus instructs us to go to them in private and share our perspective. If the person refuses to listen, we bring witnesses, and after that, the leaders of the church. Confronting in love is one of the hardest disciplines in the Christian life because it requires deep humility on our part (to take the log out of our own eyes first), and it is risky. When we dare to bring another's sin to light, we risk relationship, misunderstanding, slander, and all sorts of painful things. But if God calls you to bring up an abusive situation, you must obey, not simply for your own peace of mind, but for preventing other people from becoming victims of the perpetrator's behavior.

Refrain from chatter.

Read Galatians 5:13-15.

What does that passage warn us about?

Gossip and hearsay destroy ministries and churches. Rise above that. While it's OK to discreetly search out a discerning friend to ask for clarity and wisdom in the midst of an abusive situation, it's not OK to gossip about the situation to those who do not need to be involved. Gossip damages, but truth frees. We can be honest without needlessly "destroying one another" (Gal. 5:15).

That is not to say we shouldn't confront, but in doing so, we need to be careful with our words. If a ministry is breaking the law, report it to the proper authorities. Doing that is not gossip, it's being a responsible citizen—for the sake of those being hurt and the future damage a ministry can enact.

If attending or being a part of this body is hurting your spiritual life or damaging your family, consider stepping away for a period of time to gain perspective.

Take some time away to renew, refresh, and seek God to see what He has for you. Sometimes when you're in the midst of an abusive situation, you can't think clearly about it. Removing yourself from it for a period of time will help you clarify your position and give you time to heal. Seek out counsel outside the ministry to reorient yourself and your heart.

Keep the body of Christ in high regard.

As I mentioned earlier, God is zealous for His bride. Folks will know we're Christians by our united love for each other (John 13:35). Satan's schemes divide and bring disunity. Do not be privy to or a part of his ways. If you're deeply hurt, find a way for Jesus to shoulder that hurt. Seek counsel outside the church that's harmed you. And pray for the protection of that body. Don't contribute to its malaise.

Again, though, I must emphasize that reporting legitimate law-breaking activities is also keeping the body of Christ in high regard. It is a loving act to enact or be a part of the justice process.

Sometimes you have to permanently break ties.

If you've walked through most of these steps and still you sense God saying to move on, then do. But don't do it with fanfare or ire or angry words. Once you've said what needs to be said to the right people, leave. Spend time working through your pain. Seek counseling. Ask God for discernment for the next ministry opportunity He places before you. And also be willing to be an agent of healing for others who may leave the abusive situation.

I wish this were not an issue. But as we know, the body of Christ is made up of flawed human beings, and the potential for hurt and misunderstanding is large. What should be the safest place to process your pain and story is sometimes the opposite.

And yet, as we looked at the Acts passages earlier, there is also great potential for life change and good within the church. Let's pray our churches would become more and more like Christ as we walk through difficulties together.

DAY THREE
OUR RESPONSIBILITY

We are members of the body of Christ, and we have a responsibility to do what Jesus asks of us. While it is sometimes easy to point out flaws, we must first examine ourselves to see if we are also acting in a way that honors Christ. How are we being His hands and feet to a dying world? How are we loving the unlovely? How are we calling out sinful practices? How are we praying for those in need? How are we providing for the needs of others?

Read Psalm 139:19-24.

We tend to skip over verses 19-22. But they hint at justice and doing right by exposing those who do harm.

What can we learn from verses 19-24?

It's human tendency to easily point out the flaws in others without first looking at ourselves.

What did David encourage us to do at the end of this psalm? Why is God's inspection of us important?

As we fellowship with others, the call to self-examination is demonstrated in the sacrament of the Lord's Supper.

Read 1 Corinthians 11:17-34.

What grieved Paul's heart (vv. 18-19)? Why are divisions antithetical to the church?

Why is taking the Lord's Supper important? What does it remind us of?

According to verse 28, what are we to do before we partake of the Lord's Supper? Why do you think Paul commanded this? Why is it important to examine ourselves?

Throughout Scripture we see that God disciplines those He loves. (See Prov. 3:12; Heb. 12:4-13.) Here, we see it again in 1 Corinthians 11:32. Though uncomfortable, why is it necessary for God to discipline us?

Read 2 Corinthians 13:5.

Why do you think the apostle Paul asked followers of Jesus to examine themselves?

Recount a time when you spent time looking at your life, perhaps on a milestone birthday, or at the beginning of a new year, or at the prompting of the Spirit. What did you learn? What did God teach you?

The principle of letting God search us and convict us of sin echoes throughout the entire Bible narrative. We see Jesus talking about it throughout the Gospels.

Read Matthew 7:3-5.

According to this passage, what prevents us from being able to clearly see sin in others?

Jesus wasn't saying we never call others to account; He was saying before we do such a tender thing, we must first search our hearts as well as ask God to search our motives before embarking on a difficult conversation.

Years ago, God led me to confront a friend about gossip. The entire situation broke my heart, but before I could say one word to her, I had to go through a painful process with the Lord. He showed me my own tendency toward gossip. I became so sensitive to the subject that I couldn't even read the headlines of *People* magazine. God had to utterly break me of my own sin. And in that place of humility, I was better prepared to speak gently to my friend.

We don't talk much about biblical confrontation, but it was an integral part of the early church.

Read Jude 20-23.

This passage begins with the importance of building each other up.

Besides showing mercy toward those who are doubting, what else are we commanded to do?

We have a responsibility to look at ourselves, and we also have a responsibility to love, help, admonish, and bless others. As members of the body of Christ, we bear the weight of both. We learn to carry and relinquish burdens, and then carry others' burdens. We examine ourselves before we seek to gently call out another. This is supposed to be the normative practice of the church, but, sadly, it is often reversed.

We call out others without first looking at ourselves.

We live in the fear of others, so we never say anything—even when others are devouring the weak.

We allow sin to sneak into our hearts and our churches.

To become the kind of people friends and family members want to seek, we must heed these important commands, crying out, *Oh Lord, please look at my heart. Convict me of sin. And if there is something that needs to be discussed in my community, give me the bravery needed to speak up with humility.*

DAY FOUR
THE POWER OF APOLOGY

One of the first things we teach siblings at home is the art of an apology.
I remember modeling that behavior to my children when I messed up, so they
would internalize the language of apology. "I am so sorry for raising my voice.
I shouldn't have done that. Will you forgive me?" Seeing my children echo my
exact words heartened me.

To be a part of a thriving community is to embrace a similar ethic. We must own
up to our own sin, particularly when it has harmed another.

> **Read 1 John 1:9.**

In this oft-quoted passage, we may miss some important truths. I have always
read this, "If *I* confess my sins ..." But this is a community verse. *We* must confess
our sins together, and I would imagine that doing so would involve apology.

> Have you ever struggled with a particular sin in silence, and then found
> freedom when you confessed it to someone else? Explain.

This is the power of speaking the truth with others. In the darkness when our
struggle is confined to our head and nowhere else, lies increase; the sin has
a chance to grow cancerous, and we feel like we are possibly the worst sinners on
the planet. But confess that secret sin into the light of community? Flourishing is
the result.

Having grown up in a home where zero people apologized, I often felt like the
weight of my family's problems were all my fault. The harmony of my home
rested entirely on my shoulders. So when I had a family of my own, I made
a point to be honest about my struggles and sins so my children wouldn't
have to bear the burden I bore. It is a sheer gift to apologize. It helps others to
realize they aren't alone. It gives space for relationships. It opens the door for
reconciliation.

While we cannot force reconciliation, we can do everything necessary to create
a pathway for it. Romans 12:18 reminds us, "Do all that you can to live in peace
with everyone." That doesn't mean we can force peace through an apology.

We cannot control outcomes. We certainly cannot control others. What we can control is owning our part of a problem.

Apology has power.

Read Nehemiah 1.

Make six observations about the text, answering who, what, when, where, why, and how.

WHO	
WHAT	
WHEN	
WHERE	
WHY	
HOW	

In Nehemiah 1, we see devastation. The exiles were broken by life. They faced trouble and deep disgrace. What had protected them (the mighty walls around Jerusalem) had since been toppled. In this place of deep vulnerability, Nehemiah did something powerfully unexpected. He prayed. He confessed. He recounted the faithfulness of God.

Why do you think Nehemiah confessed corporate and personal sins?

When was the last time someone apologized to you? How did that apology affect you?

When was the last time you apologized to someone? What happened? What caused you to apologize?

The intent of apology is reconciliation—both to God and to others. Healing comes from apology, even from the kind of corporate repentance that came from Nehemiah.

Like most people, I learn best by seeing examples of this in my life. I've told this story many times, but it continues to encourage healing in myself and others.

I've been shattered in as many pieces as I've been taken advantage of: harmed, dismissed, and pushed away. I've been accused of not wanting to heal (though I've pursued healing in so many ways). When I tell my story, some recoil from it, no doubt wishing I would just be quiet and not speak of the past. Sexual abuse and trauma are painful, and the shame of those experiences thrives in darkness. One sad truth I've learned over the years is that the church doesn't like messy. The church often prefers a neat, victorious story, tied up with a cliché bow, full of manufactured piety and pasted on "joy." Seldom is there room for questions, wrestling, anguish, grief, or bewilderment—because that somehow connotes that those who were harmed are not "walking in faith."

But one man noticed me, my pain, my shattering. He changed everything for me. I met Malcolm in Cape Town, South Africa, at Cape Town 2010, the Lausanne Congress on World Evangelization. I went as one of the representatives of the United States, a humbling, surprising privilege. I volunteered to be a table host, where I led discussions with five other believers throughout the conference. We discussed what we heard from the stage—stories of redemption, persecution, and God's beautiful kingdom. We hailed from many nations: Iraq, South Africa, Nigeria, the United Kingdom, and Zimbabwe, and we each had a chance to share our stories within a circle of trust. I told my story, too.

On the last day of the conference, Malcolm, who came from Johannesburg, beckoned me. While people began taking down the props of the venue, he held my gaze. He faced me, gently touched my shoulders, and Malcolm, a man in his sixties, sunk to his knees before me, tears releasing from his ocean blue eyes. "Mary," he said, his South African accent lilting. "I need to tell you something."

I knew then something significant stretched out before me. It's one of those times I sensed the Lord say, *You need to listen. Be in this moment. Take it all in.* Malcolm struggled to keep his composure. "I apologize," he said. "I am sorry on behalf of all men for all the awful things that have ever happened to you. I'm desperately sorry."

I didn't know what to say. His words stunned me to silence. No one had ever, ever attempted to apologize for such a thing, to take on the mantle of all that sin against me—except Jesus. "Will you forgive me? Will you forgive us?"

I wept a yes his way. He stood. We hugged. And I walked away changed. Instead of excuses or dismissals, instead of tolerating always-broken me, instead of wishing away my story, instead of blaming me for my pain, Malcolm said the words that flattened my container of grief, transforming it into a dance floor, where freedom and yet another layer of healing surfaced.

We may begin the journey imprisoned. But dare to adventure alongside me, hear the echoes of the Scriptures we love so much, step into the shoes of those who have suffered, hold the hand of the One who bore the weight of every single sexual sin, and venture out onto the dance floor. Freedom awaits.[3]

May we all learn from Malcolm. May that freedom prevail in our hearts and lives!

DAY FIVE
ANATOMY OF RESTORATION

We have been learning about injured community, particularly how other people's sins and crimes hurt us. We need to know this as we love others so we can empathize with the broken and hurting. But what about the person who harms? Is there a place in the church for the one who has broken trust, who has harmed others?

The gospel plays no favorites. It is good news to both the murderer and the marginalized. We must believe this because the writer of most of the New Testament rejoiced at the murder of Christians. Saul, or Paul, encountered Jesus Christ on the road to Damascus and went from persecutor to penitent, from imprisoner to imprisoned. He proved that reformation is absolutely possible.

Let's look at the anatomy of restoration by an unnamed man in the Corinthian church.

Read 1 Corinthians 5.

Make six observations about the text, answering who, what, when, where, why, and how.

WHO	
WHAT	
WHEN	Around AD 56
WHERE	
WHY	
HOW	

What sin was the guilty accused of?

What did Paul instruct the congregation to do?

Paul used powerful contrasts in these verses: wickedness/evil and
sincerity/truth. How does allowing sin to flourish among people in
a congregation equate to wickedness and evil?

The judgment Paul instructed the Corinthians about has to do with
believers. What was he not talking about (vv. 10-13)?

Isn't it ironic that people on the outside of church today condemn it for its hypocrisy?
They see the church choosing not to address its own issues, yet heaping all sorts of
judgments on them. In 1 Peter 4:17a, we are reminded, "For the time has come for
judgment, and it must begin with God's household." In short, we must deal with the
sin in our midst, taking the logs out of our eyes first (as we learned yesterday).

Read 2 Corinthians 2:1-11.

This passage may refer to the man in 1 Corinthians 5, but many scholars think it
could be referring to an episode regarding false apostles.[4] Either way, we can learn
from this passage what it looks like when confrontation leads to repentance.

What was Paul's posture in writing about the man in sin (v. 4)?

It appears that the man chose to turn from his ways in repentance. Although this
is not always the outcome when we approach others, this man chose the way of
apology. He wept. He seemingly felt anguish over what he did.

The process for restoration is fairly simple, according to the text:

- Confront the person.
- The person repents (hopefully!).
- Forgive him or her.
- Comfort him or her.
- Reaffirm your love for him or her.

But how do you know if someone is truly repentant for his or her sins? Repentance is far more than words or sorrow. It involves action.

What actions would you expect from someone who is truly repentant of his or her sin? If it helps, think of a specific sin you were convicted of in the past and how you specifically turned away from it.

We must be cautious when someone uses repentant language. Just because someone flippantly said he or she is sorry does not mean we automatically jump back into relationship and immediately trust. Words matter little if the person continues to be untrustworthy. Protect your heart. Watch the person over a period of time. Yes, someone can be restored. That's the heartbeat of the gospel. But we must be wise in jumping back into relationship with him or her.

Pray today that you'll have a posture of repentance in your heart and life. Pray for the ability to forgive others when they repent for their actions. Thank God for His mercy and grace to forgive us.

THIS WEEK'S WE TOO MOMENT

It's been a meaty week, full of difficult subjects, particularly as it pertains to churches and ministries. To counteract that, this week's task is to find someone who is leading well. Instead of writing a card, find a way to publicly praise that person (on social media, in person, in front of others). Bless him or her for his or her faithfulness. It will encourage him or her to continue on his or her journey, and it will be a witness to those around him or her to live in a manner worthy of the gospel.

A KINGDOM PERSPECTIVE

The Bible is full of metaphors. We are to be salt and light to a dark and season-less world. God is our fountain, potter, bread, husband, rock, lamb, lion, and vinedresser. So many of Jesus' teachings are summed up in metaphoric parables—a laborer, a supper, a judge in a courtroom, and a mustard seed. These are teachings of the kingdom of God, a kingdom His followers belong to.

This week we are going to look at the shepherd metaphor in detail. What does it mean that God is our Shepherd, and since that is so, how are we to shepherd others who are hurting? We will also spend time looking at the story of the good Samaritan, a poignant recounting of love and compassion lived out.

This world is longing for a Good Shepherd. It aches for good Samaritans. As Christ followers, we are called to emulate both. As we care for others, these concrete metaphors help us understand how to carry the burdens of others.

As I write this, I am carrying a too-heavy burden. I discovered a photograph my father took of me—one he not only snapped, but painstakingly developed. It is me in the fourth grade, with a pasted-on half-smile, standing in front of a dumpster. The refuse receptacle has two words in large letters splayed across it: "MANURE ONLY."

If I were to sum up my difficult childhood in one snapshot, it would be that haunting image. What father would think it was okay for his young daughter to pose in front of such a message? It's been a month since I uncovered this image, and my heart is still breaking. I cannot reconcile it with the ever-loving nature of my heavenly Father. But, sadly, I can reconcile it with my predatory father.

As we look at shepherds and Samaritans, we will also explore their opposites—those who exploit and harm. My father's actions did not portray kindhearted shepherding.

Even so, as I carry this pain, there are others in my life, taking note of my tears. My husband is worried. My friends are praying. And encouragement is emerging from all around the body of Christ.

In this broken world, we break. Others dismiss us. Circumstances crack our resolve. Hope wanes. But, thank God, there are those who exemplify kindness and compassion. This is the power and beauty of the great upside down kingdom of God.

I cannot carry this burden alone. I wasn't meant to. I can give it to Jesus, and I can ask those who bear His name to help me carry it. It's the same for you. Our lives are not meant to be lived in sheltered isolation. We are not built to endure life alone. We are meant for community.

In my case today, family broke me. But I've also had the excruciating experience of the family of God harming me. It's been the folks in the church who have noticed that pain, shouldered it alongside me, and wept with me that have restored my hope.

Mind if I pray for you?

Jesus, oh the ache. To be hurt by someone we love is excruciating. Help us to run to You when that happens. Help us to find safe people to process with. And give us eyes to see the broken and wounded around us. Teach us to be genuine, caring shepherds. Empower us to inconvenience ourselves like the good Samaritan did. We trust You for our healing and theirs. Amen.

VIEWER GUIDE
SESSION FIVE

What do you know about lamenting? What does it mean to lament well? Do you think we lament well in our current society? Do we lament well in our churches?

Why is lamenting important?

How can lamenting help you to have hope?

How have you seen grief and joy hold hands in your own life?

Teaching sessions available for purchase or rent at LifeWay.com/IntoTheLight

DAY ONE
GOOD SHEPHERDS

We have explored good shepherds earlier through Psalm 23 and Jesus' words about them. But today, let's look at other portions of Scripture that highlight shepherds. It's important we understand the role of the shepherd to better understand how we should care for those we love.

You may not typically run into shepherds all that often, but what do you know about shepherds? What do they do?

Read Psalm 100.

Positioned in the middle of this psalm of praise is a little snippet about God and His people, using the shepherd metaphor.

How does knowing that God made us and that we are His sheep bring you hope today?

Read Isaiah 40:10-11 below.

> Yes, the Sovereign LORD is coming in power.
> He will rule with a powerful arm.
> See, he brings his reward with him as he comes.
> He will feed his flock like a shepherd.
> He will carry the lambs in his arms,
> holding them close to his heart.
> He will gently lead the mother sheep with their young.

Here we see a stark contrast (similar to the verses in Psalm 100). God is the powerful, sovereign Creator of everything we see, and yet He cares for us.

What picture do we see of God in verse 11?

When was the last time you needed God to carry you?

When have you had the privilege to carry someone else (through prayer, kindness, and/or meeting a physical need)?

Not only is God a Shepherd who carries His people and tends to their needs, but He tasks His people with doing the same.

Read Jeremiah 23:3-4 below.

> But I will gather together the remnant of my flock from the countries where I have driven them. I will bring them back to their own sheepfold, and they will be fruitful and increase in number. Then I will appoint responsible shepherds who will care for them, and they will never be afraid again. Not a single one will be lost or missing. I, the Lord, have spoken!

Here, God spoke of the exiled nation of Israel. What did He promise them?

As God raises up good shepherds, what are they tasked with doing?

What would your life look like if you were never afraid, lost, or missing?

It's interesting to note that at the very inauguration of Christ's birth we see shepherds.

Read Luke 2:8-20.

Make six observations about the text, answering who, what, when, where, why, and how.

WHO	
WHAT	
WHEN	
WHERE	
WHY	
HOW	

Why do you think it's significant that the angels told shepherds about the birth of Jesus? What kind of hope does that give you?

Alfred Edersheim helps us understand the deeper meaning behind the angels' proclamation to the shepherds:

> Somewhere deep in Jewish tradition (revealed in writings called the Mishnah), a belief had arisen that the Messiah would be revealed from the *Migdal Eder* ("the tower of the flock"). This tower stood close to Bethlehem on the road to Jerusalem, and the sheep that pastured there were not the type used for ordinary purposes. The shepherds working there, in fact, took care of the temple-flocks, the sheep meant for sacrifice.

> We can trust that God had a specific purpose for this shepherd audience, and the work they performed suggests the reason. These men who watched the sheep meant for the slaughter received a divine message about the ultimate Lamb who would take away the sins of the world through His death and resurrection.[1]

What a beautiful correlation! Our Good Shepherd, Jesus, became a Lamb who took away the sins of the world (John 1:29). He is the ultimate Shepherd because He laid His life down for our sakes. Peter and Luke promoted that same pattern as the church multiplied.

Read 1 Peter 5:1-4.

What were shepherds tasked with doing, according to this passage?

How were shepherds to lead according to verse 3?

What title did Peter give Jesus in this passage?

Read Acts 20:28-31.

In addition to feeding and shepherding the flock, what else are leaders supposed to do to protect others?

Paul's words have immediacy in this account written by Luke. Why is it important we keep watch?

How did the apostle Paul tangibly show love to those he helped?

Think back over everything we covered today as we unpacked the word *shepherd*.

List seven qualities of shepherds.

1.

2.

3.

4.

5.

6.

7.

Why are these qualities important as you care for others?

Write out a prayer that the Holy Spirit within you would empower you to love the people in your life in tangible, specific ways.

DAY TWO
BAD SHEPHERDS

The Bible doesn't always talk about good shepherds. In fact, throughout the prophetic books of the Old Testament, we see some pretty harsh judgment against those tasked with caring for the flock.

Sometimes we learn better through negative examples than positive—through cautionary tales told well.

Today we'll look at bad shepherds from Scripture to help us understand those friends and family members (and even ourselves) who have been hurt by the shepherds who should have loved and cared for them. These bad shepherds were not merely accused of neglect, but they actively abused those they were tasked with protecting.

Some experience bad shepherding in their family of origin. Parents, instead of being protectors, became those who harmed.

> Even if my father and mother abandon me,
> the Lord will hold me close.
> **PSALM 27:10**

What does this verse promise about the kindness of God?

Yesterday we read about positive shepherds in Jeremiah 23, but today we will back up a little bit and see God's chastising words toward bad shepherds.

Read Jeremiah 23:1-2.

Instead of caring, what did these shepherds do?

What does God promise to do to those who harm others?

It is clear that God is opposed to those who use His name but choose to harm others. In our church world, the line often gets blurred. We think people who are leaders should be afforded automatic trust, that as shepherds they'll care for sheep. But this verse allows for the possibility of more nefarious actions by those who claim they know God.

Read Ezekiel 34:1-24.

According to verses 1-10, what did the shepherds do, and what did they not do?

WHAT THE SHEPHERDS DID	WHAT THE SHEPHERDS DID NOT DO

The language in this passage is strong. Shepherds became predators, and God considered them His enemies.

Why do you think it breaks God's heart when people treat each other with harshness or neglect?

Verses 11-24 contain "I will" statements. Write them out below.

1. I will

2. I will

3. I will

4. I will

5. I will

6. I will

7. I will

8. I will

9. I will

10. I will

11. I will

12. I will

13. I will

14. I will

15. I will

16. I will

17. I will

18. I will

How does seeing all those "I will" statements encourage you to do the same for others?

Our actions flow from our experiences, intentions, and emotions. Our great God takes care of us when we are weak. He found us and rescued us. He welcomed us home when home seemed elusive. He grants us rest when the rat race is won. He bandages our wounds. He vanquishes our enemies with justice. He refreshes us with cool water.

Because of that, we can offer the same to the hurting in our world.

DAY THREE
A DIFFERENT ROMANS ROAD

When it comes to salvation and sharing the gospel, you may be familiar with the "Romans Road," an approach to evangelism that pulls particular verses throughout Romans to share with others about the life, death, and resurrection of Jesus and our necessary response to it. Today we will walk a different sort of "Romans Road," looking at one chapter that tells us how to live like Jesus.

We have looked at good and bad shepherds, and through that exploration, I hope you discerned that Jesus is the Good Shepherd who lays down His life for the sheep. As He is, so we must be as we live and move and breathe in this world.

But what does that mean, practically? How do we love others? How do we bear the weight of our friends' stories without bending beneath them entirely? What does it look like to love outlandishly or care for someone with abandon?

Romans 12 gives us some amazing insight.

Read Romans 12.

In order to shoulder others, we must first surrender.

What does it mean to give our bodies and lives to God?

Verse 1 in Romans 12 can be a difficult passage to read for those of us who have been forced to give our bodies to others or sacrifice our lives in many ways without consent. Thoughts of shame and guilt may spring to mind. Take comfort in the verses previous to this chapter. Romans 12 begins with an "And so," or "Therefore," depending on your translation. In chapter 11, Paul wrote a hymn of praise for our merciful God. Verse 36 says, "For everything comes from him and exists by his power and is intended for his glory. All glory to him forever! Amen."

Therefore—because of His great mercy and power—we can present our bodies and our lives, as broken and bruised and scarred as they may be, to the One who is the caring Good Shepherd, opening wide His arms to hold us and heal us. This is true worship.

We surrender by living for God's honor and glory. When we surrender our bodies, we are saying we will go where God has us go, serve as He has us serve, and obey Him with our physical abilities. When we surrender our lives, that means our entire purpose and being are aimed at serving and glorifying our merciful, powerful God.

Have you ever truly surrendered everything to God—including dreams, family, finances, health, and worries? If so, how did you feel afterward?

Can we (in our own strength) change the way we think? According to Romans 12:2, how can we possibly do that?

In verse 3, the apostle Paul talked about humility. How does humbleness help us in our relationships?

In verses 4 and 5, Paul used the metaphor of the body to refer to the church. He said, "We all belong to each other." How is this truth foundational as we seek to love the people in our lives?

According to this passage, should we boast about our gifts? What role has envy played in the church, and what role should it play?

Verse 9 says, "Don't just pretend to love others. Really love them." Who in your life exemplifies that verse?

Write out the commands in verses 9-21 in the following chart and then put an asterisk* next to the areas that you struggle with. Add a smiley face on those areas you are doing well in. I tackled verse 9 for you.

VERSE	COMMAND	HOW AM I DOING?
9	Love others; hate what is wrong	
10		
11		
12		
13		
14		
15		
16		
17		
18		
19		
20		
21		

Look over the chart you filled in. Did anything stand out to you as you wrote it out? Has the Holy Spirit challenged you to ask for help in a certain area?

What is counterintuitive about blessing people who persecute you?
How does loving that way represent Jesus?

Perhaps the most powerful verse in this passage is verse 15: "Be happy with those who are happy, and weep with those who weep."

Why do you think doing both are important?

When was the last time someone laughed with you?

When was the last time you wept with someone who was hurting?
What happened?

At the end of Romans 12 in verse 19, Paul reminded us of vengeance.

Why do you think he reminded us that it is God's job, not ours, to enact vengeance?

What would the world be like if everyone enacted vengeance against others?

You may have read this chapter of Romans and feel enlivened. Or maybe you feel stressed that you cannot do all it requires of you. Love is difficult. It involves sacrifice and pouring out. Its hallmarks are humility and taking the lowest seat, preferring others to your own agenda.

The truth? You cannot do it all. These are the actions of the Spirit within you. He gives you the ability to grow and love and help and lay down. If you feel overwhelmed, you are actually in a good place. Overwhelmed people know they need help. And the Spirit within loves to come to our help as we strive to love the people in our midst.

DAY FOUR
THE GOOD SAMARITAN

Today we're going to take a deep dive into a very familiar story. We're doing this both for us and for those who desperately need our help. Jesus told us we are to be neighbors to those around us—to love sacrificially at our own expense.

By leaving the glory of heaven and living among us, Jesus wildly demonstrated His neighborliness in the most sacrificial way. He certainly noticed the pain of humanity, our predisposition to sin, and our alienation from God and others, and He chose to rescue us. Like the good Samaritan, Jesus found us broken, bound up our wounds, and took care of us. He made a way for us to encounter God the Father by dying on a cross and resurrecting. He sent the Holy Spirit to live as our eternal Comforter.

Because of what He has done, we have hope. And we, too, can be ambassadors of hope to a dying, bleeding world.

Read Luke 10:1-24.

We begin the chapter with Jesus sending the disciples out into the harvest—the streets of the surrounding villages. He charged them with the impossible: healing the sick. He asked them to proclaim the kingdom of God to those who walked in darkness. He gave them practical advice about who to trust and how to conduct themselves in new places. He warned them they are lambs among wolves. You can almost hear the tenderness in His voice—much like the last advice sweetly delivered to a child when they leave home for the first time.

In verses 17-20, we see Jesus' warning about the spiritual forces of darkness. The disciples proclaimed, "Lord, even the demons obey us when we use your name!" Jesus answered by asserting His deity. He saw Satan's fall! He cautioned the disciples not to rejoice in the power they have over demonic influences; instead they should rejoice in their new status as registered citizens of heaven.

I have to pause a moment and simply consider the power of that truth. We are citizens of heaven! We are children of God! We are welcomed into the community of the saints! What a beautiful testimony we have as followers of Christ.

Jesus followed this by praising God and blessing the disciples (vv. 21-24).

After this, the chapter continues with a discourse between a religious law expert and Jesus. Keep this in mind: the man was not interested in conversation or learning something new. The Scripture tells us this is a test. In verse 29 it reveals that the man wanted to justify his actions. Jesus' ultimate response to his query about who our neighbor is comes in an interesting story.

Read Luke 10:25-37.

Make six observations about the text, answering who, what, when, where, why, and how.

WHO	
WHAT	
WHEN	
WHERE	
WHY	
HOW	

The "who" in this story is significant. Explain the importance of each person involved.

Religious leaders at the time were very concerned about being contaminated by anything unclean, which accounts for their actions in this story. But as we look at the story of Jesus, we see such a different dynamic. He, the ever-clean One, allowed the "unclean" of the world to touch Him. Instead of becoming unclean, He made the unclean clean. We see this same dynamic in the story. The Samaritan made the broken man whole through compassion.

The injured man was a Jew, yet leaders from the Jewish synagogue treated him as if he were a nonentity. They simply couldn't be bothered. Those who have been hurt by church leaders understand this pain. They know what it is like to have expectations that surely a leader would notice their pain, only to have the leader dismiss them.

The very leaders who should have helped chose not to. And the most unexpected person deliberately helped. We have also seen this in the sexual abuse crisis. It hasn't always been the church or its leaders who have chosen to listen to the cries of the broken, but it's been the legal system or the press who have given space for stories and healing. This should not be.

What adjective did Jesus use to describe the Samaritan? Why do you think He does this?

The priest, the "Temple assistant" (or Levite), and the Samaritan saw the man. All three had reactions—two passed on the other side, and one went to the man. Two could not be inconvenienced, but one inconvenienced himself. How does this example help you as you help others?

We are told the Samaritan felt compassion, but the narrative doesn't stop there. His compassion had legs. List what he did for the man who fell among thieves.

There is something complex about this story we don't necessarily see upon first reading. The religious man asked, "And who is my neighbor?" (v. 29). You would think the answer would be, "Your neighbor is the bleeding one on the side of the road." But no. Jesus put the religious man in the sandals of the one who is broken. He wanted him to empathize with the broken.

Then He flipped the story. "Now which of these three would you say was a neighbor to the man who was attacked by bandits?" (v. 36). The answer, we know, is the one who shows mercy. The Samaritan is the neighbor. The outsider. The despised one. The one who has been left out of the circle of community. He is the neighbor we are to love, to emulate.

The layers of this story are complex and beautiful. Could it be that those we deem unworthy are the very ones who train us how to love well? Jesus called this law-abiding religious leader to face his prejudice. He used the least likely candidate to be a hero of the story.

Friends, that's the power of the upside down kingdom. The outcasts become tutors to lead us to the heart of God. The broken show us the face of Jesus. The maligned have gifts to give us. It is not inconvenient to love others who hurt; it is essential. To be a neighbor is to welcome all to the table.

How has your reading of the text changed in light of this?

Recount a time when a broken person taught you about the nature of Jesus.

Jesus is the good Samaritan. He came from somewhere else (heaven) and was often misunderstood. Still, He pursued the broken. He loved lavishly. He is our example. In order for us to understand compassion personified, we must know Him.

DAY FIVE
THE UPSIDE DOWN KINGDOM

As we seek to love the people God has placed in our lives, we have to understand the nature of the kingdom of God. It's unexpected. It's certainly not what the Jewish people thought would happen when the Messiah graced the earth.

We live in a world where bigger is better, splash is important, and social media influencers are bent on teaching us what our priorities should be. We can easily immerse ourselves in the ethics of this world's system. Sadly, we saturate ourselves in the world's mindset far more than we study the Word of God and the way of Jesus.

And yet we see this truth: God loves the humble.

> Though the LORD is great, he cares for the humble,
> but he keeps his distance from the proud.
> **PSALM 138:6**

Who does God keep His distance from?

> As the Scriptures say,
> "God opposes the proud
> but gives grace to the humble."
> **JAMES 4:6b**

What kind of person does God oppose? To whom does He offer grace?

Today, let's look at the paradox: The kingdom is not about power, but weakness. Not about might, but meekness. We find strength only when we are emptied of it. Those whom heaven deems courageous are those the world calls small.

Read Mark 4:30-34.

There is mystery in the growth of a tiny seed. How does a mustard seed demonstrate the kingdom of God?

A seed grows buried in the darkness. Sometimes our greatest seasons of growth happen in hidden places. How has this been true in your life? How does knowing that help you endure the dark seasons?

Read Matthew 22:1-14 and Revelation 19:4-10.

What is similar about these passages? What is different?

What do both passages teach about who is welcomed into the kingdom?

Who is the one preparing the feast? Who is the feast for?

Read Luke 13:20-21 below.

> He also asked, "What else is the Kingdom of God like? It is like the yeast a woman used in making bread. Even though she put only a little yeast in three measures of flour, it permeated every part of the dough."

What does this parable teach you about the unexpected kingdom?

Read Mark 4:21-25.

How does the light or lamp represent telling the truth, even about the darkness?

What does it mean in your life today that those who have more will be given more? How does this apply to compassion?

In the middle of the Sermon on the Mount, which is a long discourse on the nature of the kingdom of God, we see the pastoral heart of Jesus.

Read Matthew 6:25-34.

What do these verses teach you about your value?

How can you convey God's care toward someone hurting today?

What are you worrying about today? What occupies your mind? What does the kingdom of God have to do with your struggle with worry?

How is it comforting to know that no matter what you're worried about, God knows what you need?

When I think about the kingdom, I realize that what is hidden is often the most important part. Those who are maligned and sent into exile are actually those who are most cherished. This helps me when I feel hidden or maligned or exiled, but it also informs the way I treat others. Knowing there will be reward for living a life that dignifies those who are hurting empowers me to endure.

This world is not all there is. The first will be last, and the last will be first. Those you expect to be heralded may end up last in line, and the quiet, unassuming saints who love Jesus in the margins may end up being heralded in the hereafter.

Loving others is our *modus operandi* of the kingdom. Don't grow weary. Keep doing the unseen work of kindness in unrecognized spaces.

The apostle Paul reminds us, "But thank God! He gives us victory over sin and death through our Lord Jesus Christ. So, my dear brothers and sisters, be strong and immovable. Always work enthusiastically for the Lord, for you know that nothing you do for the Lord is ever useless" (1 Cor. 15:57-58). Perhaps this is the encouragement you need today.

THIS WEEK'S WE TOO MOMENT

A WAY FORWARD

We need a robust view of the church, a healthy theology of what it means to be the body of Christ in a world that often feels so dark. Helping someone (and he or she helping us) is the sinew of the body. It connects us all through love, sacrifice, and prayer. How we love others is, as Jesus said, how we demonstrate our love for God (John 13:35).

Still, we grow weary. We want to give up. We long for relief—both from our pain and the pain of this world.

I have received many heartbreaking stories, the weight of which threatens to send me back to bed. This is the reality of the broken world Adam and Eve ushered in when they chose to disobey God's command and believe the lie of the enemy. This cosmic shift from Eden to a fallen world echoes today.

But in the middle of the timeline of history falls the event upon which all history pivots. God came to earth in the person of Jesus Christ, the perfect One who changed the narrative by ushering in the age of grace. This age of grace is the same one we live in today, and the one in which the church is called to minister.

Jesus' sinless sacrifice atoned for all who would follow Him down the narrow way. As those who love Him revel in the resurrection, we become agents of a new kingdom (as we read about last week). This is not a kingdom of dominion and power, but of love and life and light.

As the church, we have the unique privilege of shedding light into the dark places to love the unlovely, to herald the unheralded. Doing so helps us make better sense of our stories. It makes the pain matter somehow.

A seventy-one-year-old woman shared her heartache with me via email. When she was a child, her uncle abused her for years. She recounted how she spent most of her life stuffing her pain down inside. For decades she carried shame, feeling dirty and ignored by others. She felt unlovable. My response to her was part of the pinprick of light I have the privilege of sharing.

I wrote, "I am heartbroken by what you have endured. I am so sorry. What your uncle did to you has had lasting repercussions, and I ache alongside you. You should have been believed. You should have been protected. You should have been cherished. Justice should have prevailed. Please hear me when I type, 'You are beautiful.' I don't have your picture in front of me, but I know it down to my gut. Look what you pulled through! Look how you survived, even after such soul-crushing trauma. You carry the image of God within you, and you have survived."

I continued with some specific encouragement. And as I sent the email, I felt two things simultaneously: joy at being in the place where I could love others like this (what a privilege!) and broken-hearted sadness at the cruelty of others.

As members of the church, we, too, will battle these opposing feelings—joy at helping, sadness that helping is necessary.

Mind if I pray for you?

Lord Jesus, would You help us have the stamina, empathy, and strength to love those who are hurting? Help us be the church to those who need direction, compassion and tangible hope. We need Your strength because in our own strength we grow discouraged. Amen.

VIEWER GUIDE

SESSION SIX

Have you had a friend who lived out Romans 12 well? Share with the group.

What stood out to you about the qualities of friendship that Mary shared in today's message? Why? Which have you seen as most important in your own life?

How have your friendships helped you when you experienced hurt or trauma? What specific things did your friends do to help and encourage you during that time?

What are some practical ways, as a group or individually, to encourage others going through a painful experience?

Teaching sessions available for purchase or rent at LifeWay.com/IntoTheLight

DAY ONE
WHAT IS THE CHURCH?

The church is a called-out body of believers who follow Jesus. He is the Way, the Truth, and the Life, and He has made a way for us to be in communion with Him. He has not abandoned us as orphans. He has adopted us into His family and has given us the amazing gift of the Holy Spirit who will be our companion within for the rest of our mortal lives. We are never forsaken, never left to our own wits. He will never leave us.

In light of this, let's take a deeper dive into the church. We know from Scripture the body of Christ consists of every ethnic group, both male and female. All of humanity is represented at the foot of the cross. I had the privilege of experiencing this at a worldwide conference on evangelism in South Africa. As voices rose in hundreds of languages, I could barely stay standing. Many times, I sank to my knees, tears pouring from me at the sheer power of the redemption for all humankind.

We are both the misfits and the mighty. We are broken and whole. We are marginalized and favored. We are of the majority and the minority. But together, we make one whole. Together, we heal. Together, we experience the Lord's Supper, baptism, marriage, and burial. Together, we represent the tangible presence of Jesus on this earth.

A proper theology of church helps us endure the darkness. It empowers us to continue on. It helps us love the unlovely and see every single person as an image bearer.

Read 1 Corinthians 12:20-27.

Sum up the passage in your own words.

In a physical body, each part plays a necessary role. And certainly a body without a head cannot survive; therefore, the church absolutely needs Jesus. The two only exist in symbiosis.

My eyes need my feet to take me down the path. My stomach needs my mouth to eat. If I bring a hammer down upon my thumb, it is all I can think about. Every part matters. You matter. I matter. The person who frustrates you matters. The hurting one matters.

This passage has a powerful lesson.

What are the most necessary parts of the body according to this passage?

What are we called to do for those who are weakest in our midst?

Sadly, we often sideline the broken ones in our midst, and we revere the "put together" ones. But these verses are paradoxical. What is deemed least is what should be honored more. Paul said when we love this way, we create harmony. This is the nature of self-giving love. We pay special attention to those who are deemed less honorable by bestowing honor upon them.

The cross levels us all. I am no better than you. You are no better than me. We are all children together, loved by our Father.

According to verse 26, what happens when someone in the church suffers?

Why does the world need this kind of empathetic compassion?

Read Colossians 3:14-16.

What are we to wear every day? Why is that necessary?

Why are unity and harmony important factors in showing others Jesus?

Describe a time in the last month when the peace of Christ ruled in your heart.

When has the peace of Christ not ruled your heart? What happened?

What role does gratitude have in the way you love and serve others? How can it prevent bitterness or burnout?

When was the last time someone admonished or encouraged you? What happened? How did you feel afterward?

As the body of Christ, we represent the traits and qualities of Christ to a dying world. It is a privilege, yet it is messy. But as we understand our mission to love others, and as we grow in maturity, we become more adept at navigating this world.

DAY TWO
TOGETHER HAS POWER

As we read in Session Four, Acts 2 marked the beginning of the church. The believers couldn't help but hang out with one another. They devoted themselves to teaching. They broke bread together. They prayed. In that microcosm, people saw the love of Jesus. The world turned upside down because of the love of these new believers.

I believe we can do the same.

In isolation, we atrophy. In community, we breathe and grow and change.

But as you read these words, you may be recalling a time when a fellow believer hurt you, betrayed you, or broke you down. You may have experienced heartache because of the actions or unkind words of a leader. You may have made a vow like, "I will never trust another Christian again."

You may have erected a too-tall wall, believing that doing so would keep out the heartache, and you would be right. Walls protect us from injury and pain. But they also keep out joy.

A better way of looking at fellowship is picturing a fence with a gate. We can choose who comes in and who we can protect ourselves from. We can rightly guard our hearts from predatory people, narcissistic friends, and those who continually violate our boundaries.

With a fence and a gate, we can navigate fellowshipping with others.

With that as our foundation, let's look at the importance of community.

Read 1 Thessalonians 5:11 and Hebrews 10:24-25.

How can you encourage someone in your life to do good deeds? What does that look like?

Why do you think the writer of Hebrews encouraged believers to stick together?

Who can you encourage and build up today?

When has someone returned the favor? How did his or her encouragement change your day?

Read Ephesians 4:1-6.

How does being humble and gentle disarm people (in a good way)?

What does it mean to make "allowance for each other's faults" (v. 2)? What does it not mean?

We who have been saved by faith through grace (Eph. 2:8-9) should be gracious in our dealings with others. This does not mean we ignore all the passages we discussed in previous weeks of this study that call us to hold one another accountable for sin, confession, and repentance.

Koinonia is the Greek word used to describe fellowshipping with others within the body of Christ.

According to Bob Gilliam, "The Greek word, '*koinonia*,' was used to describe corporations, labor guilds, partners in a law firm, and the most intimate of marriage relationships. From the usage of the word, we can conclude that fellowship is a word denoting a relationship that is dependent on more than one individual. It is an interdependent relationship ... 'fellowship' was never used to describe man's relationship to God before the coming of the Holy Spirit to indwell the church. It is an exclusively post-pentecost relationship."[1]

How does knowing that we, as believers, can have fellowship with God Himself through the Holy Spirit change the way you think about God?

How does it change the way you think about His image bearers and your opportunity to have fellowship with others?

How powerful to know this type of fellowship only happened after Pentecost when the Holy Spirit was gloriously poured out. The result of this outpouring was togetherness tethered to a goal—to love others as we love God.

You cannot be a Christian only by yourself. You must experience Christ alongside others. Christianity is a communal religion, a people called out to be the hands and feet of Him to others.

DAY THREE
WALLS

Isolation creates dysfunction. Alone, we are more apt to believe lies, suffer from depressive thoughts, and entertain thoughts of suicide. Isolation is one of the enemy's tactics to render us helpless. As mentioned yesterday, when we've been hurt by others, our tendency is to build a wall—gloriously tall with razor wire circling the top—so we don't have to be hurt by others anymore.

While this self-protective act helps in the short-term, it emaciates our souls in the long-term.

When my family and I lived in France as missionaries, I literally had no friends there. In fact, the people (fellow Christ followers) I worked with acted more like enemies than friends. Each betrayal and passive-aggressive word caused me to shrink into myself. In that space of culture shock and betrayal by fellow American believers, I truly lost myself. I ceased to exist. I retreated into my shell, brokenhearted and lost.

Thankfully, God kept me from falling apart completely through my family in France and my friends back home. Both were lifelines, tethers to myself I desperately needed. They listened. They prayed. They wept alongside. Had I pushed them away, I would have been completely lost.

It does seem unfair, doesn't it? Community wounded us, and now we're asked to jump back in. How could that possibly be right?

And yet, God often demonstrates His love for us through the embrace of others. While it is important to retreat to spend time alone with Him, asking for help and meeting with Him in the darkness, eventually we must reengage with community.

But we can do so with wisdom. We learn from the brokenness and the antics of others. We discern who is unsafe and who is safe. We create that fence around us, letting in safe folks and keeping out the unsafe ones.

Read Genesis 2:18-25.

Make six observations about the text, answering who, what, when, where, why, and how.

WHO	
WHAT	
WHEN	
WHERE	
WHY	
HOW	

This was the first time in the biblical narrative when God said something was not good.

What was God's solution to Adam's loneliness?

Why is it significant God created both man and woman?

The triune God is Himself a relationship—Father, Son, and Holy Spirit. To create humankind in His image is to create what He is, a community. He exists in community, so to represent that self-giving love, He created the potential of that picture in humankind. In other words, we are more like our God when we exist in community.

Read Proverbs 18:1 (ESV).

> Whoever isolates himself seeks his own desire;
> he breaks out against all sound judgment.

Recall a time in your life when you cut even safe people from your life. What happened?

It is never easy to move beyond heartbreak. It is understandable to run away from others when they have been the source of pain. This, of course, happens in our lives as much as it happens in the lives of those we help. That's why it's important to be very careful with the hearts of others—particularly if they are afraid to trust.

One way to move forward is to see someone's evil toward you as a cautionary tale. Instead of letting it sideline you, use the pain you endured to make a holy declaration to not treat others the way you've been treated.

Growing up in an isolating home where I was often left alone and neglected, I decided I wanted something different for my family. I wanted my children to know I loved them, and I would be there for them. The negative example I endured became the catalyst to change, through the power of the Holy Spirit within.

Have you had a similar resolve, using pain you endured to make a positive change for your future? If so, describe that experience.

Another thing that helped me reengage beyond the walls was crafting a few sentences. I looked back on my story of pain and wrote honest statements about what happened to me at the hands of others. And then I wrote present tense statements about how God intersected that story. Recently, I started adding future statements to propel me forward.

Here's an example of my "I was," "I am," and "I will" statements.

PAST	PRESENT	FUTURE
I was neglected.	I am noticed by God (Matt. 10:29-31).	I will notice those who are hurting.
I was stolen from.	I am given the kingdom by God (Matt. 25:34).	I will give to those who were stolen from.
I was molested.	I am made whole by my empathetic Savior (2 Cor. 5:17).	I will help others who have walked a similar, painful path.

This kind of forward momentum empowers us to move beyond wall-making toward welcoming others back into our lives.

Your turn. Using Scripture, write five "I was," "I am," and "I will" statements below.

PAST (I WAS)	PRESENT (I AM)	FUTURE (I WILL)

Return to this chart whenever you start to dwell on the "I was" statements of the past. Consult Scripture to remind yourself of the truth of who you are in Christ and the future He has promised you. As you reflect on His promises, find ways to comfort others with the comfort you have received (2 Cor. 1:5).

DAY FOUR
SUPERPOWER

As those who help people, we are well acquainted with weakness and trepidation. We understand the holy nature of loving others, especially as we bear up under the weight of others' stories. We know we cannot do this alone. We need a Savior. We need Jesus.

The psalmist wrote of the source of our need: "My health may fail, and my spirit may grow weak, but God remains the strength of my heart; he is mine forever" (Ps. 73:26). Later, Isaiah reminded us, "He gives power to the weak and strength to the powerless" (Isa. 40:29).

I've taken two perspectives in writing this study—one of the helper who seeks to be a safe place for others, and the other of the one who is broken. You can be each simultaneously, and oftentimes, we are both helper and helpee.

Looking to the past (which could mean last week!), we can become tethered to our pain. We can begin to see our wounds as detriments, as killers of our happiness. But what if we looked at our pain, and the pain of others, in a redemptive manner? What if we saw our brokenness as our unique superpower?

The Bible brims with instances of this paradox. The weak were strong. The poor were rich. The outsiders found prominence. The broken were healers. Throughout the Old and New Testaments, we see unlikely heroes as ordinary people clothed with extraordinary strength. Let's explore this together throughout the book of 2 Corinthians.

Read 2 Corinthians 1:8-9.

What words did Paul use to describe how they felt in Asia?

Describe a time when you felt the same way. What did God do?

What was the result of this overwhelming situation? What did Paul learn to do?

Why is it we tend to learn reliance on God during difficult situations?

Read 2 Corinthians 7:5-7.

Again we see this narrative of stress. What did Paul and his companions face in Macedonia?

How did God respond to their need?

Here, we see God strengthened the weak through sending another person. Do you realize you could be the answer to someone's prayers? Perhaps God has sent you in response to someone else's desperation. Or maybe you experienced the reverse—God answered your pain by sending a "Titus" to you.

When have you been the answer to someone's prayer for help?

When has someone been the answer to your prayer of desperation?

What does this teach us about the need for community?

Read 2 Corinthians 11:16-33.

Paul listed his comprehensive (and impressive) resume in verses 21-28.

What were his "qualifications" as an apostle? In this game of "boasting," what did he share about himself?

In our churches today, there is often an unspoken expectation that if we live for Jesus, our lives should be full of good circumstances and a lack of trials. But Paul's life obviously contradicted this. Trials and pain are normative in the Christian life. Persecution should be expected. This world system, currently under the domain of a defeated foe (Satan), hates us. The enemy is hell-bent on stealing, killing, and destroying us. Sometimes we wonder why God allows so much pain, but we must understand the reality of the battle we face daily.

In what ways do you think Paul's trials were weakening him?

Of all this "boasting," what did Paul truly boast about in verse 30? Why?

What would it look like today for you to boast in your weakness?

How does this boasting-in-weakness change your perspective when helping others?

Read 2 Corinthians 12:1-10.

Make six observations about the text, answering who, what, when, where, why, and how.

WHO	
WHAT	
WHEN	Around AD 56, during Paul's third missionary journey
WHERE	From Ephesus to Corinth
WHY	
HOW	

Scholars widely agree Paul spoke of himself when he wrote of these visions and revelations.[2] He experienced heaven and Christ in ways that are unspeakable. With that kind of knowledge, he no doubt had the potential to become puffed up. But God gave him the most unusual gift—a thorn.

As he stated in the last chapter, Paul boasted about his weakness because he understood that in his weakness, he could finally feel and understand the strength of God.

After he begged God to remove this thorn (we don't know exactly what this thorn is; scholars can only speculate), God responded, but not in the way we might expect.

What was God's response?

How does knowing God's power works best in your weakness encourage you today with your own story and the stories of others?

List what Paul took pleasure (or was content) in (v. 10).

Why is it difficult for us to rejoice in painful circumstances?

The last words of this passage are powerful: "For when I am weak, then I am strong" (v. 10). This is the hope we carry as Christ followers. We don't have to have it all together. In fact, it's when we don't that we truly trust God and understand His strength.

If we are sufficient, He doesn't have to be.

If we are powerful, His power has no place to work.

If we are strong, we have the potential to strong-arm Him.

If we glory in our control, we shun His presence.

But oh, when we're weak, and we're willing to admit that weakness, then our eyes turn toward the heavens, asking for God's strength.

This is how our weakness becomes our superpower. And when our friends come to us, broken and weeping, we can remind them of this truth. Jesus said He didn't come for the healthy, but for the sick. The sick need a physician. But the healthy have no such need (Mark 2:17).

Our weakness is the gateway to God's power. And that is beautiful.

DAY FIVE
COMPASSION FATIGUE

When we help others, we tend to venture forward with gusto. Perhaps we have a little of the savior syndrome, thinking we can rescue others, or maybe we tie our worth to being a helper. Whatever the motivation in loving others, there is great potential for burnout.

The truth? We cannot change others. We can only change ourselves. But when people continue down destructive pathways, we may grow weary of the journey.

Watching the media further cements this fatigue. Wars, rumors of wars, infanticide, pestilence, trafficking, politics—all these color our outlook and contribute to deep sadness. And if our personal lives are full of issues and stresses, we grow weary.

Yesterday, we read that weakness is our superpower, but what happens when that weakness borders on burnout?

Counselor Brad Hambrick defines burnout this way: "Burnout occurs when the things that we once relied upon for life and energy become a source of discouragement and a drain. Burnout occurs when we begin to live as if caring were a necessary enemy, and we begin to prefer the 'living death' of numbness to 'caring exhaustion' of Christian relationships and service."[3]

Dan Allender, a therapist who helps many wrestle through their own pain, sees the connection between caring and burnout. "You cannot be involved at the depths of the human heart, engaging the realities of people's lives, without consequences ... You can't care and be at war for a person without having some level of wounds and scars."[4]

Lay counselor Jen Oyama Murphy writes of the cost, but also the benefit, to caring: "There is a cost to compassion and empathy. Acknowledging that does not diminish the honor and privilege it is to enter into people's heartache. But to ignore the toll that caring takes on our bodies, hearts, and minds is actually an unkindness toward ourselves and others. Intentionally receiving daily care connects us to the heart of God. He can replenish what is spent as we love and serve others."[5]

Love costs. Bearing weight costs. Intervening costs.

We pay for it somehow—often in stress, illness, and depressive thoughts. We have to learn how to disengage from others' stories so we can replenish our own. We must first be refreshed in order to refresh others. We have to drink from the abundant living water, or we will dry up, unable to offer a cup of cold water to the thirsty.

I wrote this on the cusp of burnout, so I penned it for myself, too. The weight of stories have overshadowed the glory of God. And I need rest. Do you relate?

The prophet Elijah felt that same desperation, and his came after a great spiritual victory of deliverance from the prophets of Baal.

> **Read 1 Kings 19:1-8.**
>
> What caused Elijah to flee?

How is it helpful to know great opposition often comes after great deliverance? How can you better prepare yourself the next time you see victory in your life or the life of the one you are helping?

In a short period of time, Elijah moved from joy to utter despair. Has this happened to you? Someone you are walking alongside? Why do you think this happens?

What was God's response to Elijah's state?

Sometimes we simply need to eat and sleep, to rest from what is bothering us. We need sustenance and hope. A simple acronym may help you as you struggle: HALT. It stands for Hunger, Anger, Loneliness, and Tiredness. It's a helpful inventory to take.

- Are you hungry? Have you been eating well? Healthily?

- What is causing your anger? Anger usually is a reaction to fear. Peel it back. Why are you angry? What is really bothering you?

- Are you lonely? In today's world, we're surrounded by people offline and online, but we still feel the sting of isolation. Maybe you need some good one-on-one time with a trusted person.

- Has weariness overtaken you? Are you sleeping enough? Is the rest you're taking actually restful? There's a difference between blankly staring at a screen and truly finding life-giving pursuits.

If you are feeling any of these four things, consider it one of God's ways to slow you down, to feed you, and encourage you to rest, just as He did with an overwhelmed Elijah.

Both Jesus and His disciples faced soul tiredness. Let's read about how Jesus dealt with compassion fatigue.

Read Mark 6:30-52.

Make six observations about the text, answering who, what, when, where, why, and how.

WHO	
WHAT	
WHEN	
WHERE	
WHY	
HOW	

The tired disciples returned from their missionary trip. They shared their victories and worries with Jesus. But instead of jumping right back into helping others, Jesus instructed them to retreat to a quiet place. He modeled and invited rest. We see similar retreats throughout the Gospels where Jesus went to an isolated place to pray.

After the great victory of feeding the five thousand, Jesus sent them off on a boat, came to them on the water, told them not to worry, and then calmed the storm.

What do we learn about retreat from this passage?

Since people mobbed Jesus and clamored for His attention, why is it significant He felt it necessary to find a quiet place?

Sometimes I find it hard to take care of myself. I immerse myself in the cares of others, neglecting me. It helps when I realize Jesus died for me, too. I am worthy of protection, favor, and help. I, too, am loved by God. And He is wooing me toward rest. He makes that invitation to us all. Rest and rejuvenation are the gifts we give ourselves and those we love.

As we close out the personal study, take time to pray. Thank God for His power in your weakness. Thank Him for providing rest and an example in Christ. Ask Him to comfort you as you comfort others. Ask Him for the eyes to see those who are hurting and the boldness to share the hope of Christ as you minister.

THIS WEEK'S WE TOO MOMENT

Contact someone in the study and connect with her in real life—wherever you want, however you want.

THE SUPERPOWER OF WEAKNESS

VIEWER GUIDE
SESSION SEVEN

Does it encourage you that your weakness is also your superpower? Why or why not?

How does your own weakness enable you to encourage others?

How has God used your weakness to give glory to Him?

What is one takeaway you have from the video teachings during this study?

LEADER GUIDE

LEADER GUIDE

Thank you for taking on the responsibility of leading your group! I know you will be blessed and challenged as you lead this study. Below, find some tips to help you effectively lead the group study times.

FORMAT

GATHER: This is a time to greet and welcome everyone and then to get them talking. In each session, you're provided a list of questions to help participants review the previous week's personal study. Feel free to adapt, skip, or add questions according to the needs of your group.

WATCH: Each week you'll show a video teaching. Encourage participants to take notes on the Viewer Guide pages in their Bible study books.

DISCUSS: During this time, you'll help the participants debrief what they've heard on the video teaching. A list of questions is provided on each session's Viewer Guide page. Again, feel free to adapt, skip, or add questions as needed to foster discussion.

PERSONAL STUDY: Each session contains five days of personal study to help participants dig into God's Word for themselves. The final day of each week features a "We Too Moment" to help participants act on what they've learned throughout the week of study.

PREPARE

STUDY: Make sure you've watched the teaching video and completed each week's personal study before the group session. Review the discussion questions and consider how best to lead your group through this time.

PRAY: Set aside time each week to pray for yourself and each member of your group.

CONNECT: Find ways to interact and stay engaged with each member of your group throughout the study. Make use of social media, email, and handwritten notes to encourage participants. Continue these connections even after the study ends.

A WORD OF CAUTION

This study is a bit different than most in that it focuses not only on our personal spiritual lives, but also the health, pain, and trauma of others. In light of the subject matter, keep the following recommendations in mind:

- There may be a tendency for group discussion to drift into a counseling session. Talk with your pastor or ministry leader about resources and counselors in your area to refer women to.

- Pray. Ask the Holy Spirit to be in control of every conversation and to give you wisdom and discernment to lead effectively and compassionately.

SESSION ONE

GATHER

Welcome the group to the study and distribute Bible study books to each participant.

WATCH VIDEO SESSION ONE

Play the video for Session One. Encourage participants to take notes or jot down questions on the Viewer Guide page.

DISCUSS

Use the questions found on page 12 to debrief the video teaching and get to know one another.

SESSION TWO

GATHER

Welcome women back to the study. Use the following questions to review last week's personal study and prepare for the video teaching.

- What did you learn about Hagar this week? How did her story encourage you?

- Recount a time when God intervened in your life. What happened?

- Read 2 Corinthians 1:3-7 as a group. Who comforts us in our pain and worry? Why do you think so?

- As light bearers, what is our responsibility in terms of the darkness?

- Read Matthew 5:3-10. How does reading this passage through the lens of suffering change your experience of Jesus' words?

WATCH VIDEO SESSION TWO

Play the video for Session Two. Encourage participants to take notes or jot down questions on the Viewer Guide page.

DISCUSS

Use the questions found on page 48 to debrief the video teaching.

SESSION THREE

GATHER

Welcome everyone to Bible study. Use the following questions to review last week's personal study and prepare for the video teaching.

- What stood out most to you in this week's study?

- If someone were to ask you, "What is the gospel?," what would you say? How would you explain it?

- Which of the qualities of a safe person comes easily to you? Which do you need to work on in order to be a safe person for others to entrust their stories with?

- Read Romans 12:15. Why do you think Paul included this verse in the Romans 12 narrative? Why is it important to weep with those who cry out?

- When has God brought comfort into your life?

WATCH VIDEO SESSION THREE

Play the video for Session Three. Encourage participants to take notes or jot down questions on the Viewer Guide page.

DISCUSS

Use the questions found on page 80 to debrief the video teaching.

SESSION FOUR

GATHER

Welcome the women back to the study. Use the following questions to review last week's personal study and prepare for the video teaching.

- Looking at the story of Tamar as a cautionary tale, how should we not respond to someone who has been traumatized?

- Think about who you know that might be going through a crisis or responding to trauma. How can you be like Ruth in his or her life—encouraging, offering sympathy, and helping point him or her to Christ?

- Read Matthew 6:9-13. Think through the questions you answered about Jesus' prayer. Which one had the biggest impact on you? Explain.

- When have you longed to have soul rest? Are you in that place right now? How does knowing Jesus is pulling the bulk of the load help your perspective?

WATCH VIDEO SESSION FOUR

Play the video for Session Four. Encourage participants to take notes or jot down questions on the Viewer Guide page.

DISCUSS

Use the questions found on page 108 to debrief the video teaching.

SESSION FIVE

GATHER

Welcome the group back to the study. Use the following questions to review last week's personal study and prepare for the video teaching.

- What struck you about this week's personal study? Explain.

- Read Acts 2:42-47 as a group. How do we see these same things happen in church life today?

- Read Psalm 23 together. What are qualities of the Lord in this passage? In other words, what does a shepherd do?

- What actions would you expect from someone who is truly repentant of his or her sin? If it helps, think of a specific sin you were convicted of in the past and how you specifically turned away from it.

WATCH VIDEO SESSION FIVE

Play the video for Session Five. Encourage participants to take notes or jot down questions on the Viewer Guide page.

DISCUSS

Use the questions found on page 134 to debrief the video teaching.

SESSION SIX

GATHER

Welcome the group back to the study. Use the following questions to review last week's personal study and prepare for the video teaching.

- You may not typically run into shepherds all that often, but what do you know about shepherds? What do shepherds do?

- How does knowing that God made us and that we are His sheep bring you hope today?

- Look over the chart you filled in on page 147. Did anything stand out to you as you wrote it out? Has the Holy Spirit challenged you to ask for help in a certain area?

- What stood out to you about the story of the good Samaritan? Recount a time when a broken person taught you about the nature of Jesus.

- Why do you think it breaks God's heart when people treat each other with harshness or neglect?

- Who has acted like a good Samaritan in your life?

WATCH VIDEO SESSION SIX
Play the video for Session Six. Encourage participants to take notes or jot down questions on the Viewer Guide page.

DISCUSS
Use the questions found on page 162 to debrief the video teaching.

SESSION SEVEN

GATHER
Welcome the group back to the final session of study. Use the following questions to review last week's personal study and prepare for the video teaching.

- Read Colossians 3:14-16. What are we to wear every day? Why is that necessary?

- Describe a time in the last month when the peace of Christ ruled in your heart.

- How does knowing that we, as believers, can have fellowship with God Himself through the Holy Spirit change the way you think about God?

- How does it change the way you think about His image bearers and your opportunity to have fellowship with others?

- If you feel comfortable, share one or two of your "I was," "I am," and "I will" statements with the group.

- Read 2 Corinthians 12:1-10. How does knowing God's power works best in your weakness encourage you today with your own story and the stories of others?

WATCH VIDEO SESSION SEVEN
Play the video for Session Seven. Encourage participants to take notes or jot down questions on the Viewer Guide page.

DISCUSS
Use the questions found on page 185 to debrief the video teaching.

CELEBRATE
Celebrate what God has done in and through your group during the past seven sessions of study. Pray together about further steps God may be asking you to take as a result of the study and make plans to follow up with one another.

ENDNOTES

SESSION ONE

1. [...]l Kynes, "God's Grace in the Old [...]estament: Considering the *Hesed* of [...]he Lord," *Knowing & Doing: C. S. Lewis Institute*, 2010, accessed January [...]6, 2020, https://www.cslewisinstitute.org/webfm_send/430.

2. James Orr, ed., *The International Standard Bible Encyclopedia, Vol. 2*, s.v. "Hagar," (Chicago: The Howard-Severance Company, 1915), 1,316.

3. Matthew George Easton, "Ishmael," in *Easton's Bible Dictionary, Bible Study Tools*, accessed December 16, 2019, https://www.biblestudytools.com/dictionaries/eastons-bible-dictionary/ishmael.html.

4. Mary DeMuth, *We Too: How the Church Can Respond Redemptively to the Sexual Abuse Crisis* (Eugene, OR: Harvest House Publishers, 2019), 41–42.

5. Ibid, 42.

6. L. Lewis Wall, "Jesus and the Unclean Woman," *Christianity Today*, January 13, 2010, accessed December 16, 2019, https://www.christianitytoday.com/ct/2010/january/17.48.html.

7. Strong's G2899, *Blue Letter Bible*, accessed December 26, 2019, https://www.blueletterbible.org/lang/lexicon/lexicon.cfm?t=kjv&strongs=g2899.

8. Frank Viola and Mary DeMuth, *The Day I Met Jesus: The Revealing Diaries of Five Women from the Gospels* (Grand Rapids, MI: Baker Books, 2015), 136.

9. *Merriam-Webster*, s.v. "theology," accessed December 16, 2019, https://www.merriam-webster.com/dictionary/theology.

10. *Encyclopedia Britannica*, s.v. "Concepts of life after death," accessed December 16, 2019, https://www.britannica.com/topic/Christianity/Concepts-of-life-after-death.

11. Strong's H6755, *Bible Hub*, accessed December 16, 2019, https://biblehub.com/hebrew/6755.htm.

12. Ibid, DeMuth, *We Too*, 82.

13. Charles Spurgeon, "The Stony Heart Removed," No. 456 (sermon), delivered May 25, 1862, accessed December 16, 2019, http://www.romans45.org/spurgeon/sermons/0456.htm.

14. Ibid.

15. Ibid, DeMuth, *We Too*, 83.

16. *Merriam-Webster*, s.v. "eschatology," accessed December 17, 2019, https://www.merriam-webster.com/dictionary/eschatology.

17. Ibid, DeMuth, *We Too*, 46.

18. "What is the kenosis?," *Got Questions*, accessed December 17, 2019, https://www.gotquestions.org/kenosis.html.

19. Ibid, DeMuth, *We Too*, 49.

SESSION TWO

1. Martin E. P. Seligman, "Learned Helplessness," *Annual Review of Medicine, Vol. 23* (February 1972): 407–412, https://doi.org/10.1146/annurev.me.23.020172.002203.

2. Mary DeMuth, *Not Marked: Finding Hope and Healing after Sexual Abuse* (Rockwall, TX: Uncaged Publishing, 2013), 62–63.

3. George Wigram, *Englishman's Concordance*, "*paraklēseōs*," *Bible Hub*, accessed December 20, 2019, https://biblehub.com/greek/parakle_seo_s_3874.htm.

4. Strong's G3875, *Blue Letter Bible*, accessed January 7, 2020, https://www.blueletterbible.org/lang/lexicon/lexicon.cfm?t=kjv&strongs=g3875.

SESSION THREE

1. Diane Langberg, as quoted in Philip Monroe's article, "Must Read: Diane Langberg on 'Trauma as a Mission Field,'" *Musings of a Christian Psychologist*, June 20, 2011, accessed December 27, 2019, https://philipmonroe.com/2011/06/20/must-read-diane-langberg-on-trauma-as-a-mission-field/.

2. *Merriam-Webster*, s.v. "trauma," accessed December 27, 2019, https://www.merriam-webster.com/dictionary/trauma.

3. "About Child Trauma," *The National Child Traumatic Stress Network*, accessed February 24, 2020, https://www.nctsn.org/what-is-child-trauma/about-child-trauma.

4. Ibid, Seligman.

5. Strong's H7965, *Blue Letter Bible*, accessed January 9, 2020, https://www.blueletterbible.org/lang/lexicon/lexicon.cfm?t=kjv&strongs=h7965.

6. "*wašōmêmāh*," from *Englishman's Concordance, Bible Hub*, accessed January 9, 2020, https://biblehub.com/hebrew/veshomemah_8076.htm.

7. Ibid, DeMuth, *We Too*, 41.

8. Ibid, Strong's H2617.

9. Strong's H4755, *Blue Letter Bible*, accessed January 31, 2020, https://www.blueletterbible.org/lang/lexicon/lexicon.cfm?t=kjv&strongs=h4755.

10. Kerry Howley, "Everyone Believed Larry Nassar," *The Cut*, November 19, 2018, accessed December 30, 2019, https://www.thecut.com/2018/11/how-did-larry-nassar-deceive-so-many-for-so-long.html.

11. Ibid, DeMuth, *We Too*, 24.

12. Strong's G4043, *Blue Letter Bible*, accessed January 7, 2020, https://www.blueletterbible.org/lang/lexicon/lexicon.cfm?t=kjv&strongs=g4043.

SESSION FOUR

1. Ibid, DeMuth, *We Too*, 210.

2. Mary DeMuth, "10 Ways to Spot Spiritual Abuse," *The Website of Mary DeMuth*, accessed January 8, 2020, https://www.marydemuth.com/spiritual-abuse-10-ways-to-spot-it/.

3. Ibid, DeMuth, *We Too*, 28.

4. David E. Garland, *The New American Commentary: 2 Corinthians, Vol. 29* (Nashville, TN: B&H Publishing Group, 1999), 118–132.

SESSION FIVE

1. Alfred Edersheim, "Why Did the Angels Announce Jesus's Birth to Shepherds?," *Christianity.com*, April 13, 2010, accessed January 14, 2020, https://www.christianity.com/jesus/birth-of-jesus/shepherds-and-angels/why-did-the-angels-announce-jesuss-birth-to-shepherds.html.

SESSION SIX

1. Bob Gilliam, "3. The Importance of Fellowship in a New Testament Church," from *The Measure of A New Testament Church, Bible.org*, May 26, 2004, accessed January 17, 2020, https://bible.org/seriespage/importance-fellowship-new-testament-church.

2. Matthew Henry, *Matthew Henry's Commentary on the Whole Bible (Concise)*, "2 Corinthians 12," 1706, via *Bible Study Tools*, accessed January 17, 2020, https://www.biblestudytools.com/commentaries/matthew-henry-concise/.

3. Brad Hambrick, *Burnout: Resting in God's Fairness* (Phillipsburg, NJ: P&R Publishing, 2013), 8.

4. Dan Allender, *The Allender Center*, "Vicarious Trauma and the Church," March 22, 2015, accessed January 17, 2020, https://theallendercenter.org/2015/03/vicarious-trauma/.

5. Jen Oyama Murphy, "The Cost of Caring," *Christianity Today*, November 5, 2015, accessed January 22, 2020, https://www.christianitytoday.com/women-leaders/2015/november/cost-of-caring.html?paging=off.

ENDNOTES   191

More from Mary DeMuth

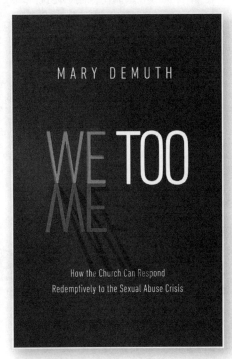

WE TOO

"Timely and necessary... This book is not only a warning. It is an opportunity. An opportunity to live out the gospel we so passionately proclaim. And it starts with listening."—J.D. Greear, President of the Southern Baptist Convention

Time's Up: Addressing the Unspoken Crisis in the Church

We like to think the church is a haven for the hurting. But what happens when it's not?

Author and advocate Mary DeMuth urges the church she loves to rise up and face the evil of sexual abuse and harassment with candor and empathy. Based on research and survivors' stories, along with fierce fidelity to Scripture, DeMuth unpacks the church's response to sexual violence and provides a healthy framework for the church to become a haven of healing instead of an institution of judgment.

In the throes of the #MeToo movement, our response as Christians is vital. God beckons us to be good Samaritans to those facing trauma and brokenness in the aftermath of abuse and provide safe spaces to heal. DeMuth advocates for a culture of honesty and listening and calls on the church to enter the places where people are hurting. In the circle of that kind of empathetic #WeToo community, the church must become what it's meant to be—a place of justice and healing for everyone.